ROUGH BEAUTY

Forty Seasons of Mountain Living

Karen Auvinen

SCRIBNER

New York   London   Toronto   Sydney   New Delhi

Scribner
An Imprint of Simon & Schuster, Inc.
1230 Avenue of the Americas
New York, NY 10020

The timing of some events in addition to certain names
and characteristics have been changed.

First Scribner hardcover edition June 2018

SCRIBNER and design are registered trademarks of The Gale Group, Inc.,
used under license by Simon & Schuster, Inc., the publisher of this work.

For information about special discounts for bulk purchases,
please contact Simon & Schuster Special Sales at 1-866-506-1949
or business@simonandschuster.com.

The Simon & Schuster Speakers Bureau can bring authors to
your live event. For more information or to book an event, contact the
Simon & Schuster Speakers Bureau at 1-866-248-3049
or visit our website at www.simonspeakers.com.

Interior design by Kyle Kabel
Watercolor illustrations by Greg Marquez (artquez.com)

Manufactured in the United States of America

1   3   5   7   9   10   8   6   4   2

Library of Congress Cataloging-in-Publication Data is available.

ISBN 978-1-5011- 5228-3
ISBN 978-1-5011-5230-6 (ebook)

For my mother, Susan, who did not have a voice,
and for Greg, who helped me find mine

and one knows,
after a long time of solitude, after the many steps taken
away from one's kind, toward the kingdom of strangers,
the hard prayer inside one's own singing
is to come back, if one can, to one's own,
a world almost lost, in the exile that deepens,
when one has lived a long time alone.

—Galway Kinnell

Contents

CONTENTS

ROUGH BEAUTY

The Hard Prayer

M arch was thick with anticipation—the pendulum between winter and spring, between dormancy and growth—the month of hope, the month of change. Its arrival meant winter was certain to end. By then, I'd had nearly four and a half months of cold and isolation. And although I loved the quiet—days that were meditative and curving, nights that were icy and full of dreaming, and the kind of luxurious deep sleep that comes when you're wrapped in layers of blanket and down—that didn't mean it was easy. Snow fell a foot at a time. Silence was a presence; sometimes my own voice broke the stillness like a body crashing through ice. The snap and plunge startled me. And then there was the winter wind, the yang to the yin of snow, which howled and clawed at the cabin, rattling the glass panes like a live thing. Inside such a landscape, you learn to stay put.

By March, I was ready to emerge.

Driving home that morning, I glanced up through the slender bodies of lodgepole pine, a silhouette of trees against an impossibly blue Colorado sky. A few crows trailed the hillside, scouting for trouble. The birds reminded me of packs of teenage boys—loud and rowdy and full of themselves. It was early still, perhaps 10:00 A.M., and chilly, the first day of March. I'd built a fire in the woodstove of my cabin, where nighttime temperatures inside dipped into the low fifties, and sautéed chopped celery and onion for corn chowder before I'd gone out to deliver mail on a rural route, one of three part-time jobs. Elvis, a handsome blond husky mix and my constant companion, sat in the seat of the old blue 4Runner next to me, nosing the cold mountain air through a crack in the window.

I was thinking about spring, the change of season. Despite years of mountain living and the fact that I should have known better, my whole body buzzed with thoughts of warmer, longer days, hummingbirds whirring at my deck, the smell of rich dirt rising from the softening earth. The first real glimpse of spring—pasque flowers shocking the russet landscape with pale purple—would not come for another six weeks, but I allowed myself to be hypnotized by the sensation of *thaw*. I could feel it in the stiffness of muscles and limbs, the paleness of my skin. My body was ripe for release. In just a few weeks, I'd head out for the equinox in Utah to celebrate the return of sun and let my winter self unknot and loosen her grip.

This winter had been full of firsts: I'd finally settled into a home after too many awkward years of moving from place to place; I'd finished the last of three college degrees; and I was gloriously alone, without the economic necessity and relative instability of house-mates. I had only myself to annoy or answer to. After over a decade of the roller coaster of odd jobs and school, I'd come to rest at last.

Here, I told myself, was where I would begin. In settling down for the first time in my life, my commitment was not to a person but to a place. Forgoing the possibility of job offers in other states or the economic comfort of a nine-to-five life, I placed my bet on landscape, putting all my chips on wildness.

I'd landed on one of the highest habitable places on the apron of the Front Range of the Rockies that still offered Internet access and a reasonable (fifty-minute) commute to the nearest city (Boulder). The Bar-K cabin stood at 8,500 feet, where the winters were long and the summers brief, but glorious. There were a handful of neighbors spread across the mountain, most settled on one- to two-acre lots kept private by uneven terrain dotted by lodgepole, kinnikinnick, and currant bushes. Another few hundred people lived in Jamestown, four miles down-canyon, where I'd lived for a few years when I'd first gotten Elvis and now cooked at the Mercantile Cafe, the town's one and only business. I wasn't living in the wilds of Alaska, but the relative isolation and solitude of living "up top" suited both me and my semiferal dog, who behaved far better without fenced yards and leashed walks. We were both a bit untamable. I had an instinctive need for distance and space. Like the grizzly bear, an animal that once inhabited the Great Plains of Colorado, I needed room. Plus, I'll take the overblown perils of living with bear and mountain lion over the more menacing threat of people any day, the quiet and loneliness of mountain living over the noise and stimulation indigenous to the modern world.

Through the fall and winter, I'd been putting down roots. I was drunk on the idea of autonomy and quiet living, not to mention at long last being able to make a home exactly *how* I wanted it. I bought chunky Mexican wood chairs for the living room and invited friends for tequila shrimp or Thai curry. I shelved my books according to type and genre. There was a meditation space in the long narrow bedroom and a place to do yoga. I even wintered my first herbs— tricky on my shady patch of dark pine forest—and began planning a lettuce garden for the deck in summer. I fed the birds, throwing out seed for juncos, and hanging long slender tubes for chickadees and woodpeckers, birds who were bullied by Steller's jays and camp robbers (gray jays), not to mention one determined gray squirrel, who chattered angrily at everyone. Mornings, I sipped coffee and watched the shifting hierarchy while I wrote and Elvis studied the squirrel through the sliding glass window, his ears up and head cocked to the side.

Living wild succinctly arranges priorities: You make food, take shelter, stay warm. Seasons and weather dictated every aspect of my day, from what I was eating to what I was doing. In winter, I hibernated on the mountain and ate braised meat and root vegetables over polenta or potatoes and spent long days reading by the fire and writing. In summer, I hiked and made picnics with sliced tomatoes and hummus, fresh berries and whipped cream, and reveled in glorious afternoons out of doors with Elvis: Nature ordered my days.

Winter meant I built a fire each day in the cold belly of a massive cast-iron stove that heated all four rooms of my house and prevented the pipes from freezing. The cabin didn't have propane or electric heat, so each morning, I'd go out barefoot in the snow to gather kindling in a bucket and then lay the sticks over crumpled newspaper stuffed between two parallel logs inside the stove. I built the fire tipi-style between the logs to get a good flame and then lay a few larger pieces of pine over the top, waiting to add the best fuel—thick oak blocks cut from railroad ties. Fire building requires patience—you have to feed the embers bit by bit. Too much large fuel too soon and the wood gutters and smokes. Too little air and the flame dies. I'd usually start the fire with the stove doors open and then close them to a crack to let the air draw up the chimney, making coffee and feeding Elvis while I waited until it was ready for smaller oak chips and then larger blocks. The routine felt like a ritual, equal to meditation or the ritual I had of writing down weather and birds each morning. It was my way of keeping track, taking stock, laying the foundation for the day to come. Now it feels like a prayer for a life I never could have imagined.

Part of what kept me living up there were the jobs I juggled: Besides teaching writing at a community college near Boulder, I had the postal route, a twenty-five-mile loop that took me through two canyons on a wide circle around my cabin, in addition to the Merc job in Jamestown. Going to town every day was impractical, so like a lot of people, I picked up work on the mountain.

That morning, I let the day fly ahead with the crows: There were papers to grade, an essay I had been working on. I turned my truck onto Crockett Trail and the forest closed in as I glanced toward home. Inexplicably, something glowed on the rise where the cabin sat; the trees nearby were lit by warm light, the same lovely, eerie light a campfire casts in the woods. A voluminous orange cloth covered the deck on the west end of the cabin. Against logic, I wondered if the landlord was fumigating. The cloth swayed elegantly in the morning air, forming scarlet and orange ripples that flicked and snapped.

It took a second for the picture to make sense.

My home was on fire. The thought slammed into my chest.

I stomped on the gas pedal and smashed my fist into the truck's horn.

Once my brain had formed the word *fire,* I swerved down the dirt driveway directly across the road from my cabin, honking my horn. My neighbor, Barbara, a brunette with a big laugh, appeared waving her phone: She'd already called the volunteer mountain fire department—ten minutes ago. She dialed them again. She and her husband, Chuck, had a property management company, and my lot, within eyeshot, was one of the rentals they took care of. I'd known them for six months, long enough to know I wanted to keep my distance. They were friendly but drank too much and talked loudly about their guns, their rights, their freedom. Chuck slurred his words even when he wasn't drunk.

"I don't know where they are," Barbara said, but I was already backing toward my house.

Time stuttered and broke, unfolding in slow motion and jerky, time-swallowing shocks. Even now, images flash: my truck jolting to a stop twenty feet from the fire; Elvis watching quietly, calmly from the front seat; my hands waving in the air near the deck as if I could put the fire out with their motion; me running for the hose that was already burning.

The first rule of fire is to move away, but the instinct to save both the pieces and proof of my existence was automatic. I ran toward the fire, toward the heat, inexplicably, thinking of the rent check I'd written out that morning and the first new top I'd purchased in months hanging inside my closet with its price tag still on. Fire rolled and tumbled in great waves from the front room onto the deck to the west with the steady systematic roar of a train, the same sound a tornado makes. The house had long north and south faces, and the fire was concentrated in the northwest corner, near the front door and the woodstove, and along the deck on the west side. Flames tongued the gas grill and a half-full tank of propane on the deck. Beneath, a pile of old scrap wood would catch at any moment. The deck burned audibly; the cracks and pops pierced the roar. Inside, a wall of flame advanced through the long tunnel of the house toward the rear and my office.

The last tenant had had a chimney fire, I remembered suddenly, a little sick. They were not uncommon on the mountain, where so many homes were heated with wood. But all winter, my mantra had been "I'm careful." I'd had the chimney swept in the fall, and my primary fuel—oak—burned clean and hot. Dimly, I recognized my own smugness as part of a collective lie people tell themselves: "That won't happen to me" is the thin glass between safety and danger, the illusion of control held against a messy, unpredictable world.

I ran to the east end, thinking of my computer sitting on my desk just four feet inside the back door. The fire had progressed only a quarter of the way through the cabin, sending flames into the living room and threatening the kitchen. There was still time. I could save the most important thing. So I opened the back door.

The second rule of fire cautions against entering a burning building. But I was already cataloging what work could be lost: two books of poems, a collection of short stories and a book of essays I'd been working on, countless notes and fragments—all on my computer. Of course I didn't have a backup, a fireproof box, a disk stored in my truck or somewhere else. We always imagine disaster happening *to someone else*. Even though every writer I'd known whispered the horror of Hemingway's lost stories in shuddering tones, I somehow felt immune to catastrophe—though I'd survived plenty of them in my life.

The door sprang free in my hand and a blast of black smoke kicked me back off the rear porch. I stumbled, coughing, and caught myself on the ground thirty feet away, pounding it with my fist, yelling, "No! No! No! No!" as if I could stop what was happening, as if I could extinguish the fire with the strength of my arm hammering the earth and the will of that one thought: *STOP*.

This can't be happening shuddered across my brain. I was sobbing now, great, gut-wrenching cries rising from the deepest part of my body. But there were no tears, only wails surging from me, like thunder, the sound made in the atmosphere as ions and elements rush back together.

Now I had broken the third rule of fire: I'd left the door open, and cold mountain air poured into the house, feeding the blaze. More thick black smoke gushed out, billowing across the dry winter ground. The bird feeders were empty, the sky clouded over. I moved away, back to my truck, and drove it across the road to Chuck and Barbara's, leaving Elvis inside while I went to watch the fire from my driveway.

An eeriness set in on the mountain. A kind of disjointed silence. The world went perfectly still: Except for the constant thunder of fire, the woods were marked by an absence of sound. No birds calling or squirrels chattering, no shouts, no gathering crowd. I stood alone, waiting for the fire truck. It began to snow.

Chuck appeared in his SUV honking his horn too. He dragged a hose toward the house, but the spigot on the outside of my cabin was gone by then. Then he headed off to the Left Hand Volunteer Fire Department firehouse, five miles away.

"They should be here," he said.

Donna, who lived about fifty yards to the west and was my only visible neighbor, appeared and then disappeared to warn anyone else who might be home along Crockett and then Bridger, the road behind ours. Because of lot size and the roll of the mountaintop, neighbors might not know; in the dry late winter, sparks from the fire had the potential to catch and spread quickly. After Donna had knocked on his door, my neighbor to the south, a man I didn't meet until later, opened the curtains in the back of his house to flames visible between the trees that separated us. *Holy shit*. He stared incomprehensibly, he would tell me later, astonished he hadn't heard a thing.

9

Meanwhile, I waited, feeling something beyond helpless. The fire pushed into the middle part of the house, its advance through the windows like the slow pull of a fiery train through a station. Each window in the long north face of the house represented a room: Now the fire filled the bay window off the kitchen. I knew the massive farm table made of solid oak I'd saved so long for was burning. I tried not to think of things, but against my will, my brain popped with pictures of objects I'd collected through hard work and luck: an Indonesian wood dresser that I'd been given, the professional KitchenAid mixer I'd gotten at cost, and the three hundred or more cookbooks I'd collected as the buyer for the largest brick and mortar cookbook collection in the country, the Posturepedic mattress set my mother won for me in a raffle.

But the real grief was my writing. Only the bathroom lay between the fire and my office. Eight feet to go.

I began a kind of prayer.

"Just not my hard drive, not my hard drive," I chanted, under my breath, invoking gods, angels, the spirit of everything I could imagine. It's funny how clean my priorities, how simple salvation had become. I began to horse-trade with the cosmos: *Take it all*, I thought. *Leave me my words.*

"Come on, come on," I whispered.

Fire is the two-edged sword of mountain living. The smell of woodsmoke marks winter days in thin columns rising from chimneys in Jamestown and homes dotted across the mountain. It's the scent of comfort and warmth. In Celtic mythology, the goddess Brigit guards the triple fire of healing, metallurgy, and poetry. Her fires transform and create.

But fire can also destroy. Jamestown had been threatened by wildfire just six months before, in October, when a late-autumn squall zigzagged up and down and across the canyon, making dustdevils in the road all night long. Trees shimmied like sparklers and wind howled into the morning when a gust sheared a tree that fell on a thirteen-thousand-volt power line. At first reported under control, the fire later blew up with a resurgence of wind, racing down Porphyry Mountain toward town. My friend Karen Z, along with other Jamestown residents, was happily carousing with mimosas and breakfast burritos at the Merc while the owner, Joey, poured free coffee when the sirens went off. They had minutes to pack and flee. Jamestown firefighters made a heroic effort to save the town, digging trenches on its borders and setting back-fires to ward off the wall of flame that came within feet of homes along the town's northern edge. Karen's house was safe, as was every home in town, but over twelve "official" structures on top of Porphyry Mountain had been consumed, homes that were off the grid, without electricity and water. The slurry bombers had not arrived in time.

The day of the Jamestown fire, I walked out to the overlook just five minutes from my cabin and watched the wind shove the fire toward the plains east of me. It was moving away, pushing smoke toward the eastern horizon. And I was above it all. Still, I packed my truck just in case, taking Elvis' bed and his food, my camping gear and winter shell, my notebooks, some photographs, my chef's knife, and my desktop computer.

I wanted to be prepared.

I thought about that day as I watched flames appear in the cabin's bathroom window, my bedroom behind it. Two feet to go. My fists were balled into the sleeves of a too-thin fleece jacket. I crossed my arms over my chest and shoved my hands into my armpits. Shivering, I rocked back and forth on my feet to keep from crying. My nose dripped with cold. I watched the fire from somewhere outside my body. And waited.

Well over an hour after the initial call, a command truck arrived with just two people. Almost immediately, they got stuck in a ditch trying to back down the incline of my driveway onto the incline of the muddy road in three inches of slick, wet snow. A second fire truck had to pull them out to clear the road. Finally a third truck arrived. It was almost noon.

I ran from firefighter to firefighter imploring each to get my computer out. But a computer is not a baby, nor even a pet. *Please help me.* My request was shrugged off. "Go ask the chief," someone said. I was begging for a thing, an object—but that object was my life, my identity.

Finally, Karen arrived. Almost twenty years older, she had long been my camping and dog buddy. We were known in town as "the Karens"—she was Karen Z, I was Karen A. We had a prickly relationship—her blunt style matched my own—but we traveled well together—*two trucks*—and had forged a friendship over favorite camp spots and early-morning walks with our dogs.

"My computer," I wailed, and she set off in search of the fire chief, a man named Denison, while I watched the assembled crew stand and watch the fire. They cut power lines and a few adjacent trees and waited for a water truck to arrive.

By now, word of the fire had spread down the mountain, and a few of the Jamestown hoard—those people who were hard-core drinkers and talkers at the Merc and appeared, invited or not, at every Jamestown birthday, retirement, and wedding—gathered outside Chuck and Barbara's to watch. They laughed and bullshitted, passing a bottle of Maker's Mark from lawn chair to lawn chair. Chuck held a hose in his hand. The fire was another occasion for a party, I thought dimly. I hated them all.

"Want some?" asked JoJo, a gray-bearded Cajun and one of Jamestown's "dirty old men," tilting the bottle toward me. "Good for what ails you." He nodded at the house. He'd lost his house in the Overland Fire that previous fall and was now living with his wife on Main Street smack in the middle of Jamestown.

I tipped the bourbon to my lips. The burn provided no warmth, no comfort. Then, I wandered back up the road to see what was happening and passed another couple from Jamestown walking hand in hand as if on their way to a picnic.

"Hey, Karen," called Richard, as if we'd both come for the same reason. He was a handsome sixtyish musician I knew as a regular from Saturday nights at the Merc, which is to say we could identify each other in a lineup and offer one or two unverifiable stories we'd heard, but that was about it. Only weeks later would he sidle up to me while I was working at the Merc and sheepishly give his condolences.

The fire crew began pushing in the walls of the cabin, their first decisive action. They said words like *contain* and *surround and drown,* instead of *save* and *salvage.* A steady jet of water shot from a hose into the center of the house. Its purpose was to keep the fire from spreading to nearby homes. Later someone would tell me the joke about the Left Hand VFD: Their motto: "Saving foundations since 1975."

My isolated corner of the mountain was crowded now. Bodies moved in the snow through the landscape—firefighters with axes and hoses, neighbors edging up for the best view. I thought of Sylvia Plath's "peanut-crunching crowd," and there I was: the incidental performer of a striptease. Finally, Karen Z ushered me toward Carly's house, a place uphill seventy-five yards to the east, where I was given a mug of tea and a pad of yellow legal paper. There were other people there too, drinking coffee. Karen was on the phone with Victim Assistance.

"Write down everything," Carly said, handing me a pen.

Later that night in a motel room paid for by the Red Cross and unable to sleep, I would obsessively list all that I had lost: the nineteenth-century Finnish confirmation Bible that belonged to my great-grandmother Auvinen—my only family heirloom—a broadside given to me by the poet Kate Braverman, who'd composed a poem for me on its face. Signed first editions. My mind stopped. I'd never be able to replace any of it. Instead, I listed things whose value had a bottom line, things that might be purchased again—all related to cooking, all painstakingly collected: rare, out-of-print cookbooks by Jacques Pepin and Anne Willan; All-Clad pots and pans; a full set of professional German knives; the oak table; hand-thrown imported-Italian plates, stacks of retired Fiesta ware. I filled five pages, line by line, feeling guilty about my love of color and beauty: an exquisitely set table with contrasting plates, good orange and gold linens and sparkling green glass; sleek platters that elegantly showed off food.

I hadn't grown up with nice things. *Perhaps I hadn't really earned them,* I would think, and that's why they were gone. I would not be able to shake the feeling that I was at fault somehow, that I'd done something to deserve what had happened. That night, I counted every expensive object I could think of, estimating its dollar value because I simply couldn't estimate the value of things whose price was measured by memory or the heart.

At Carly's, people swirled around, sipping coffee and talking, but I was outside it all, in shock. I didn't want to talk or listen to or be near anyone. I think I might have left abruptly, disappearing suddenly. It was afternoon. Snow continued to swirl in fat flakes; winter was not yet done. The fire crew wandered the incline around the cabin like silent priests. I didn't have it in me to watch until the bitter end. I turned my back and slid down the bank to Chuck and Barbara's and my truck, opening the door and letting Elvis out to stretch his legs. He'd been waiting since midmorning and all through the fire without so much as a whine. He hopped out, sniffed, and made a beeline for a bank of snow. Dropping, he rolled onto his back, legs flung wide, and wiggled back and forth, grunting. Above us, the front room of the cabin suddenly collapsed, metal roof hinging like a door.

I looked up at the house, blinking, and then down at my dog joyously rubbing himself with snow.

*   *   *

For months, my home was a giant grave. The site would not be cleaned up until early summer. People from the neighborhood told me stories about charred paper scattered by wind—pieces of my journals, my stories blowing like snow across the mountain. My writing haunted the landscape.

"Should I save them for you?" asked one neighbor I'd scarcely known.

"No," I said. It was too much.

She'd cornered me one night at the Merc to tell me how she had made poems from the fragments. I know she thought the idea would please me, but I wanted to choke her. Those words were mine.

My instinct had always been to roll up my sleeves and get on with it, however grim the task, and into this familiar terrain I retreated, putting miles between me and what happened. *Must have been meant to be*, I thought. It was the only answer to the question *Why?* The only answer that could dredge hope from tragedy, reason from two feet of ash.

Later, when I looked at pictures taken of the fire, I would see a home glowing with contained light. The thick walls and metal roof kept the fire *in*. From a distance, the blaze through the trees looked radiant—cheery almost—as if my home was a giant woodstove. Indeed I was told the inside temperature reached one thousand degrees.

My cabin had become a kind of kiln.

Only a few things emerged: a cast-iron fry pan; my favorite pottery mug embossed with the sun, the moon, the stars; and a bear fetish made from pumice. All forged by fire. Nothing else within the two feet of ash and metal inside the cabin's charred footprint was salvageable—even my computer. I'd hopefully retrieved the steel box, but it was too late: The hard drive had dissolved into a pool of shimmering metal. For days, I puzzled over the shapes and forms I unearthed; I was an anthropologist, sifting through the debris of my life.

Nearly forty, I'd scrapped and punched my way to the present moment; it had taken me years to build this fire. What remained was misshapen: my own skin and bones, the years I'd spent walking away, mistaking opposition for independence. It had all led me here. Fire had been with me from the start—it had a hand in my own making. Memory and grief were like ash. At first, in the months after I watched my cabin burn, the hard prayer was for survival. *Let me live.* Only later, after I had retreated further, becoming intimate with rocks and stars, letting landscape cover me, would I see that it was also my return.

PART I

Marlboro Woman

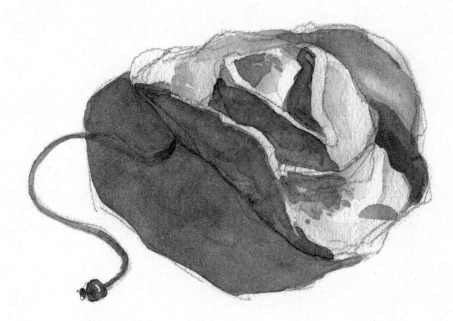

Chapter 1

Good Girl

My grandfather Pete, a second-generation Italian immigrant with large capable hands, used to tell a story about me sitting on his lap eating waffles when I was two. When he lifted a forkful of buttery, syrup-glazed sweet to my mouth, my lips parted baby-bird-like. "Zoop, that waffle was gone!" he'd say. "And I'd give you another and 'Zoop!'" he teased. When he wasn't fast enough, I grabbed waffles with my fists.

"Zoop! Zoop!"

Although he laughed and told the story over and over, it was clear from his bemusement that I had somehow broken the rules.

That appetite landed me on the outside of what passed as appropriate for girls in my family. My taste for life extended well beyond food; I had a tendency to charge at the world, to take it all in. "My little bull," Barbara, my petite pearls-and-diamonds grandmother, called me. My knees were always scuffed, my elbows rough and dry, my shoulders and feet too big, my hair full of knots. I wanted to rub up against things but lived under an umbrella of expectation: Why wasn't I more refined? More girlie? I licked the sidewalk because

I liked the taste of dirt, and I dug up worms after a strong rain so I could watch them tunnel and wiggle in the plastic tub in the garage where I kept them. I was certain the world held mystery and I yearned to gather it by the fistful. When I was four, I jumped up and down on my parents' bed in front of the vanity in our Sunnyvale, California, trailer, telling my mother one day I would leap into the mirror and go live with the little girl I saw there. Later, I raced invisible friends on roller skates around the outer elbow of the Bay Area cul-de-sac where we lived for a few years, kicked around the West by my father's Air Force career: me; my brothers, Chris and Steve, who bookended me in age; my parents; and our dog, Mitzi.

"Go put your clothes on," Grandpa Pete shouted, as I ran naked through his house at age three, five, seven. Such exuberance was troubling.

Once, lamenting that I was the opposite of dainty, Barbara, who never stopped trying to coax my hair into curls and my hands into my lap, stretched my fingers into a chord on a *toy* piano I'd gotten for Christmas and exclaimed, "These hands, these chubby little hands!" as if the shape of my limbs was a character flaw for which *I* should be accountable.

My future appeared in the form of two dolls I was given: one, a nun in a black and white habit, the other, a bride, dressed in veiled white lace. I placed both quietly in their boxes on a shelf in my bedroom until the day I chopped the head off the bride for an art project and buried the nun in the backyard.

I hated dolls.

Even though I saw women burning their bras on the nightly news, my family, led by the old-world swagger of my Italian father, remained impervious to the social revolution whose epicenter was a mere fifty miles up the Bay Area coastline from our first house. Instead of hippies and Haight-Ashbury, I knew about Vietnam and the Zodiac Killer, a faceless monster I worried haunted the bushes on my way to school.

We had moved to Milpitas, California, located off the Nimitz Freeway at the "stinky exit"—so named because the air was thick with the peaty smell of cow manure and salt marshes—just before I began elementary school. The hills were rolling and green, if always vaguely obscured by fog and—even then—smog. Our gold stucco house tucked inside the last court on the edge of the housing development was palatial compared to the trailers we'd lived in— first in Nevada, where I was born, and then in Sunnyvale, where my father was later stationed. For the first time, we had our own washing machine and dishwasher, and my father made much of the fact that he'd gotten to choose not only the color of the house but the avocado-green appliances and two-toned shag rug. We were coming up in the world!

I learned to roller-skate and ride a bike on Moon Court, playing for hours alone with my cartoon friends, Marine Boy and Little Audrey. Girlfriends were scarce. I had only Irene, a blue-eyed beauty from Texas who lived next door, but she was several years older. She had long lashes and dark hair that curled slightly around her freckled face and was Texas polite, saying "yes, ma'am" or "sir" to my parents. She invited me over to play dress-up with her Dawn dolls, the shorter, more glamorous version of Barbie, but I couldn't sit through more than one costume change, even though I longed for Dawn's hot-pink evening gown with the sparkly silver bodice.

No matter how hard I tried to cajole her, Irene wasn't interested in running or riding bikes or fishing for crawdads in the ditch out back with me. Instead she instructed me on the qualities of a lady, once telling me if I was too proud of my long hair, gremlins would come in the night and chew it off.

This left the other kids on the block—all boys—who wanted to play either chase or doctor, and my brothers, who forged an alliance over G.I. Joes and Army games and model airplanes, bonding over anatomy and naming their penises Mortimer and Charlie. They kept a "pee bank" in the scrap pile on the side of the house in a Mr. Clean bottle. I tried once to make my own deposit, squatting among wet lumber and mud over the narrow bottle opening with predictable results.

In my family, women were parsley on the plate—accessories or helpmates: My grandmother Barbara, a slim beauty with Betty Grable legs, was the elegant accompaniment to my grandfather's powerful presence; my mother sailed through her life behind a cloud of Salem smoke, always tired. Lethally silent. The adult child of two pugnacious alcoholics, she had learned from an early age to stay out of the line of fire, and denied her own profession by parents who refused to pay for college because she was female, at eighteen she joined the Air Force, where she met my father, "Wally Cakes." I believe he was the first man she ever kissed. By twenty, she was married, pregnant, and discharged from the service. Back then, you could be career military or you could have kids. Mom quietly followed my father's Air Force career from California to Nevada and back before moving to Colorado and Hawaii, all the while working one dead-end retail job after another to help the family make ends meet.

I don't have one solid memory of her from those early years. Instead, all I have is a collection of images: my blond mother holding up a frilly baby-blue nightgown at Christmas when I was six; Mom in cat-eye glasses standing in front of an Easter ham decorated with pineapple and cherries when I was seven; Mom, neat looking in the shag du jour, posing in a light blue dress suit with her parents in front of a mission in Monterey. But these are photographs from the family album. In them, my mother is a static figure, captured mid–half smile, frozen in time. And that's how she was at home: a bug under glass. I watched for years as she was pressed flat under the weight of my father's volatile personality.

"Go put your face on," my father shouted at her. He harangued, then menaced. Eventually, a decade into their union, he hit.

Dad was handsome, with pouty lips and a shock of black hair combed back from his face. No wonder my mother fell for him. He was larger than life and charismatic, but unpredictable—charming in one instant and boiling mad the next. No one knew when things were going to blow up.

*   *   *

The stories of my family are the stories of men. I grew up in the shadow their larger-than-life selves cast, coveting the pleasures of gusto and sheer masculine joy. Each lived with the kind of prerogative and independence I would be denied. Plainly put: Men did things, women watched. Their escapades were the mythology of my childhood: tales of my great-grandfather Bernardo, a giant at six feet eight, who guarded the Italian King Umberto and later mined diamonds in Africa and was alleged to have killed two men who tried to rob him by crushing them together inside the circle of his massive arms. He'd come to America with my great-grandmother, who would die during childbirth, and moved out west to mine coal in Utah, later dying of consumption.

Or Pete, Bernardo's son, a Depression-era urchin who survived starvation at an orphanage by eating bugs off the walls and, at fourteen, herded sheep in Utah. He spent long days and nights in the canyon country near Bryce on horseback, a dog and big blue western skies as his only companions. From an early age, I was haunted by the story of him alone in the wilderness and yearned for that kind of adventure.

My father's tales were of his misadventures, consisting largely of the naughty things he'd done on his uncle's Wyoming ranch or to earn a ruler across his hands in Catholic boarding school in the forties. During a lesson on hell, he raised his hand and asked the nun if, after he died, could he go live with the devil? It sounded more fun.

One of his favorite pranks was to take us through the drive-thru, ordering in a mock Chinese accent only to switch to a swarthy Frenchman or a daft Dutchman at the window as my brothers and I giggled.

Once I tried to emulate my father's bravado, dramatically telling him a joke going around school about the little red wagon. I reached the punch line, pleased with my performance, giggling uncontrollably, until my father shook me by the shoulders and told me the joke was dirty, forbidding me to speak to or play with the *nasty little girl* who'd told it to me.

Left out of the family heroic narrative and lacking someone to look up to, I developed an instinct for going it alone. I would do it all by myself. Just five and unable to tell time or read, I knew that when *Sesame Street* ended in the late morning, it was time to go to school. My mother had already left for work by the time I picked up my Josie and the Pussycats lunch box and went to wake my father, who was sleeping off the graveyard shift of a second job. Then, I walked the mile to school.

If I was good . . . I thought, because good was the best thing I could be. Trouble was, being a *good girl* meant not only being obedient and polite but, most impossibly, being pretty. I was plain and a bit chubby. My front teeth met in an arrow-like point; my smile was an awkward apology. When my dad, who liked to imagine he could see into the future, prognosticated about his children, he said Steve would be an astronaut, Chris a scientist, and I, he'd proclaim as if bestowing the best gift, would be "Miss America 1982." He might as well have said I'd grow up to be a horse or a swan. His prediction wasn't necessarily a vote for my beauty; instead he was imagining the best, most successful thing I could be.

Caught between the competing desires to be a good girl and to get in on the action, between acceptance and rebellion, I zigzagged through my early years like a deer stuck inside a fence. I so often fell short that I thought *I must be bad,* taking as evidence that I'd once hit my grandmother in the face when she sweetly leaned down to kiss me good night. Her late-night embrace had startled me.

"Oh! Well!" she harrumphed, walking away. Mortified, I aped ignorance when she inquired the next day, "Honey, you didn't mean to hit your grammy, did you?"

Determined to correct my wickedness, I decided what I lacked in traditional good-girl looks or patience I would make up for in obedience. If I couldn't be one kind of good girl, I'd be another. Once, promised a whipping by my father when we got home, I dutifully retrieved the belt myself and handed it to him.

But adherence to the laws of my family provided only passing relief. A larger institution promised greater reward: the Catholic Church. The church was the place of a perfection so sweet that saints shimmered with golden halos and my irreproachable grand-father teared up every time he worked his fingers over his black pearl rosary. I wanted to be just as saintly, just as virtuous. When I'd learned in catechism the story of a girl who'd seen a baby in the road and pushed it out of the way of an oncoming car only to die—but die a good Catholic—I was constantly on the lookout for people and animals to save at my own peril. The fact that my dying seemed to make the act holier made it all the more desirable. After I was told good pious Catholics crossed themselves when they passed a church—*any church*—I began the practice at seven. Instinctively, I'd come to understand that my lot was to *convince* others of my virtuousness. So I dutifully said the half dozen Our Fathers the priest gave me for confession after he'd lectured me in the dark closet of the confessional about "honoring thy father and mother," even though I hadn't mentioned Mom or Dad, or confessed to defiance. I had obedience down.

My sins were lies and greed.

I stole Neapolitan coconut candy from the store for the fifty-cent Saturday matinee until the day my father caught me and hauled me screaming "No, Daddy, no!" up the aisle to the store manager, who I swear had a cop on hand who showed me his handcuffs and said he could take me away and I'd have to spend the night in the clink. Another time, I convinced my older brother, Chris, already a guilt-ridden child who carried the heavy expectation of being firstborn, that he had broken the washer lid by climbing on top of it.

And, I liked to tell stories.

At show-and-tell, I excitedly displayed the seashell figurine I'd gotten on Fisherman's Wharf or the strange Easter basket made from a hollowed-out bleach container, topped with a rubber Mother Goose head, lining up my special items weeks in advance. But once I ran through my repertoire, I made things up. I reported with glee that Mitzi, our spayed half basset hound–half German shepherd, had had puppies that wiggled and whined and slept like little balls of brown and black dough curled up against their mama's white tummy. Another week it was our nonexistent cat, Midnight, who'd had a litter and kittens that were mewing all over the house. Still later, my mother was pregnant with twins. I don't know why I saw birth as the answer to my state of affairs—it hadn't worked out all that well for me.

*   *   *

On the weekends, my brothers and I did what my father wanted to do: fish, go to the base to watch the fighter jets in air races, bet on horses, bowl, see the newest sci-fi film, scour rose beds and parks in Sacramento for the *Bee*'s annual treasure hunt, where my father was sure *This year!* we'd be the ones to decipher the weekly clues and find the object that proclaimed us the "lucky winner!" of a huge cash prize. Dad was certain that his big payout was just one bet, one stroke of luck away.

My father, who boasted he couldn't get lost in the woods, was a born outdoorsman who hunted elk and deer. Above all, I loved camping and fishing with him. Our trips were expeditions in which Dad packed the station wagon full of coolers and sleeping bags, aluminum chairs, fishing poles, our fifty-pound tent, and always, a huge batch of spaghetti he'd spent the entire day making. I learned to shoot a .22 and gut a trout and spot deer. Nature, I understood, was simultaneously glorious and dangerous. At night, inside the thick skin of our canvas tent, I'd lie awake breathless, half-terrified, half-awestruck that I couldn't see my hand waving just inches from my face, and imagine my fingers drifting like stars in the night sky while my dad sat by the fire on bear watch with Mitzi and a .30-.30, sipping Crown Royal.

When morning came, there would be fried trout and rosemary potatoes and sunny-side-up eggs cooked in bacon grease for break-fast with blackened campfire toast as smoke drifted through the forest. My brothers and I combed the campsite for claw marks and overturned rocks from the bear my father scared away or deer and rabbit tracks in the mud.

On those trips—the only vacations my family would have—my father filled our heads with stories about trolls who moved around at night but turned to stone during the day, or an island-size bass that lived in a lake we fished. Whenever we saw the island that was the bass' gravel and shrubbed back, I swore it had shifted spots. I would grow up to tell stories of my own, in Girl Scouts and later as a camp counselor during college: ghost stories about the "albinos" or the bucket-headed man who lived among trees. Even though the tales were meant to scare, I understood that out there, beyond streetlights and pavement, things were different.

My father's favorite pastime was "to go see the horsies" at Bay Meadows on the days when my mother worked. I remember watch-ing palm trees sway across the track and drinking soda while Dad and his friend Uncle Stan drank bourbon and Coke from frosted cups and talked in code about each race. The track grounds smelled of cigar smoke and were littered with faded yellow and blue and red tickets—a color for each place and type of bet—and my brothers and I picked them up looking for accidentally discarded winners. Bettors roared, "Come on, seven! Go, three!" The announcer trilled the "Daaaay-leee Duuuuub—ble!" along with the sound of the track bell. Between races, I turned the language of the track over and over in my head: *exacta, win-place-show!, trifecta,* and my favorite, *quinella,* a beautiful word that sounded like a luscious dessert made with vanilla ice cream and some kind of elaborate cake. Dad held his race book tight in his hand and made notes with a pencil while studying the odds board before he placed his bet—always at the last minute—while I picked my winners by looks—a combination of silks and color of the horse—a method that on at least one occasion would have earned a huge payout and propelled Uncle Stan to buy my picks for the next three races.

I recall my father's friends, a gang of Air Force guys—all young, all in their twenties—almost more than I can recall my own. There were the "Uncles": Stan was a card player with thick black glasses and clearly the brains of the bunch, who called my brothers and me "critters." Don had a blond Afro and a funny way of flicking his fingers when he talked. He would eventually marry my mother's sister, Mary Ann, and become my real uncle. Last was Aunt Paul, a sweet man whose given name was Lester, nicknamed Aunt by me because we already had too many uncles. Larry Harmoney was the big redheaded guy who once vomited on the juniper in the front yard during one of my dad's *bagna càuda* parties, causing it to turn gold and double in size. He shot the ducks and pheasants we roasted for Super Bowl Sunday, the kids put to the task of plucking the scalded carcasses. At the center of the group was my father, a man who bowled with a butterscotch-colored ball inscribed with the word *polata*, Piedmontese slang for testicle, and had a bag of dirty jokes for every party.

Because Dad was the sun around which so many orbited, my brothers and I were often left, moonlike, waiting for his return. I've waited at ball fields and dog races, outside grocery and department stores, in "kids' areas" at casinos with a handful of quarters for games and snacks while my parents gambled the afternoon away, and at other people's houses while my dad played bridge or watched football and drank Carlo Rossi and Gallo red burgundy by the gallon with his friends, singing "Aye-yay-yay-yay, suck my *juan-nachee*."

Huge chunks of my childhood yawn with boredom—not the generic kid kind where we'd complain, despite toys and friends, of "nothing to do," but the kind developed in killing time. My brothers and I made up a game called Bridge-Break-Alligator-Eat for those days Dad left us in the car while he shopped for groceries at the base commissary—"Only one kid allowed in at a time!" he'd say, and that meant he'd simply leave us all, rather than pick one to go inside. In the game, the person acting as the bridge spanned the divide between the front and back seats of our station wagon while the "break" crawled across his back. The alligator waited in the foot space of the backseat, all of us chanting, "Bridge break alligator eat!"

Dad was our master of ceremonies at home too, declaring that we were going to Dairy Queen or the drive-in. "Put your pajamas on, get your pillow," he announced, emcee-like. In our house, he was head cook and doctor, pulling teeth with a pair of metal pliers and a handkerchief, a bit of bourbon rubbed on the gums.

He was also our drill sergeant.

On Saturdays, my brothers and I woke early to try to get in as many cartoons as we could before my father started yelling orders. Armed with Windex and paper towels, a broom and the vacuum, we cleaned the house, the garage, our rooms, performing our appointed tasks dutifully. If we didn't work fast enough and with enthusiasm, Dad threatened and bawled.

"Move!" he'd say. And we jumped to. Menace was Dad's management policy. All he had to do was snap the belt or threaten to give us "something to cry about," sometimes turning one of us over his knee, pants pulled shamefully down. As we grew older, the belt was increasingly replaced by his massive hand.

While my father proudly relayed the story of how I potty-trained myself when I was less than a year old, I only remember seeing Dad standing over my older brother, yelling at him "to go to the bathroom" at the end of the long hallway in the Sunnyvale trailer. When Chris hesitated, my father's hand snaked out and slapped his two-year-old son. I'd barely begun to form words, but I recognized danger, and instinctively avoided the need to be taught.

One such lesson concerned matches. As my father tied a rubber band around my pinched fingers and placed a lit match at the center, he demanded: *Are you going to play with matches again?* "No, Daddy!" I cried. He kept at it, staring at me with gold-flecked green eyes not unlike my own. The flame crept down the wooden stick. The heat began a slow burn on my fingertips. "No, Daddy, no, Daddy!" I screamed.

Love was punishment.

* * *

By the time I'd entered third grade, well before the apricot and cherry trees my parents planted in the backyard had matured enough to bear fruit, my father was transferred and my family moved from Moon Court in Milpitas to Poteae Drive in Colorado Springs, where the wide Colorado sky and edge-of-the-prairie existence swallowed me. I could imagine no more beautiful sight than the snowcapped mountains rising to meet the sky from the wide bowl of the grasslands in winter, or the veils of shadows they cast in the summer.

My parents bought a split-level house in Cimarron Hills, my fifth address, surrounded by empty, weed-filled lots in a sparsely built edge of the development lined with rolling fields that stretched toward Kansas.

By fifth grade, I had become a Goody Two-Shoes, a model student, diligent, attentive, helpful—the teacher's pet—and a Girl Scout, earning merit badges as a Housekeeper, Observer, Dabbler, along with those in Home Health & Safety, Hospitality, and Water Fun, but all that would change as I increasingly felt like a Victorian heroine locked in the drawing room while I watched the lives of my brothers with a curious mixture of rage and envy.

They earned money with a shared paper route and Chris went out for football, while Steve played Little League baseball. Their chores were outside—they mowed the lawn and weeded, they walked the dog. Me? I babysat, a job that consisted of killing time. My chores ranged from mopping and polishing furniture to cleaning the bathroom—"girl stuff."

In Boy Scouts, my brothers went on camping trips and slept in a tent, while in Girl Scouts, I learned to square dance and make paper flowers for people who lived in the old folks' home. Before our troop went on a cookout in the woods, we spent weeks making a "sit-upon," a pad tied by strings around the waist so we wouldn't get dirty when we sat on the ground. Inspired by those early camping trips with Dad, I dreamed of sleeping alone in a pup tent and tracking animals in the woods. I wanted to learn to whittle and cook biscuits over a campfire and identify plants.

As soon as I joined Girl Scouts, I began begging my parents to send me to summer camp, where I would live in the woods for a week and become a real woodswoman, but there was never enough money. *When I was twelve,* they promised.

In the meantime, I'd climb the hill on the lot to the west on early-summer evenings when the sun slanted across the fields and bats twirled recklessly in the darkening blue sky to sit in the dirt at the quieting of the day. Tall weedy sunflowers and Russian thistle, plants that would dry out and tumble end over end only to gather on wire fences on windy autumn days, crowded my wide shoulders.

I was sure I'd landed in the wrong family.

The hot day exhaled, when suddenly, a strong hum, like air blown through a long tube, like a radio coming suddenly into tune, filled my ears. It was not the first time I'd heard the sound. I closed my eyes and held my breath, lifting my head hopefully to the sky.

What I told myself was this: Long ago I'd come to earth with my alien family—my *real* family—and I'd gotten lost or separated, but then time had run out and they'd had to go back home. Somehow, I'd found my way into this family—people who too often regarded me suspiciously or with bewilderment and openmouthed shock. *What's she doing now?*

I knew the sound in my ears was the voice of my kin, people who were just like me, trying to tell me how to get back home—only I'd forgotten the language. If I concentrated, I told myself, I would remember. If I held my breath, the words would come. And so I remained perfectly still, digging my fingers and toes into the cool earth as the first stars appeared in the sky, and tried to remember the language of my birth.

*   *   *

My mother went back to school to study art—the profession she'd hoped to pursue when she was eighteen—and suddenly the house was alive with her projects: sculptures carved from plaster molded into milk cartons and wire mobiles hanging from the ceiling. Mom played Elton John's *Goodbye Yellow Brick Road* and Jim Croce and danced with me in the living room. She bought me my first pair of bell-bottoms and taught me how to macramé. She painted a metal watering can yellow and dotted it with flowers for the garden and planted corn and zucchini out back.

My parents fought more.

One day, out of the blue, my father asked me how I would feel about having a baby sister.

"I've always wanted a sister!" I gushed.

A few days later, my parents broke the news: We would be a family of six.

But my childhood fantasy that new birth would make my life more exciting turned out to be like gulping down a cold glass of milk only to find it had soured. I was thrilled at the prospect of a new sibling, sure she was a girl, and I eagerly watched as my mother's stomach blossomed into a big ball.

My sister's birth was difficult for my mother, who had high blood pressure and, at thirty-five, was considered high risk. She had to be hospitalized at the Air Force Academy. For two and a half months, I waved to Mom through the window of her room because my father said kids weren't allowed on the ward. In the end, Nancy was born a squalling child—only five pounds, five ounces—and difficult to calm down, as if sensing just exactly where she'd landed.

I turned twelve three weeks before she was born.

There would be no Girl Scout camp. Instead, the summer before junior high, I was the designated babysitter, simply adding one more item to my list of chores inside the home, as I fed and changed and played with my sister while my parents tried to repair their marriage through counseling and in a series of evenings out.

I had gladly accepted the responsibility of my sister—it made me feel important, adult. No one questioned my default position as nanny, not even me at first, but before long I knew I was trapped. I'd devoted years to trying to be a good girl, to anticipating the needs of others, doing as I was told. Where, I thought, had it gotten me?

That summer, as I watched my brothers, free to ride their bikes or visit friends while I sat with Nancy, something in me broke.

That's when I decided to stop.

The decision was like a bomb detonating in my head. After too many years of acquiescence, of *yes*, I would begin deliberately, defiantly to say *No*.

Chapter 2

Saying No

In junior high, I was determined to carve out a tiny patch of ground at our small farm school east of Colorado Springs. At the end of my first year, on a whim, I tried out to be a cheerleader, squeaking in as an alternate before working my way to the main squad. My defining move? I could yell the loudest.

Suddenly hot to be away from home and my babysitting duties, I went out for track, unsuccessfully running long distance (I didn't pace myself) and the hurdles (not fast enough), and then for the gymnastics club. Although outright spunk and the nimble ability to launch into backflips and handsprings got most girls invitations, my solid footing and stubbornness did it for me. I was unshakable on the balance beam and could do the splits even though I didn't have any real gymnast tricks in my repertoire. Still, what I lacked in finesse and body type I made up for in guts and determination. My signature move on the uneven bars was the death drop, a dismount where I threw myself backward from a sitting position on the lower bar. My torso rotated upside down around the bar and up, so that when my chest rose, my back was to the bar and my legs dropped solidly to the floor, arms lifted. I harbored the fat girl's need to prove herself to everyone. I'd push harder, I'd be stronger, I wouldn't quit. Out of this resolve rose the new bud of confidence, and for a brief time, I was one of the popular kids. All that would be abruptly cut off when we left Colorado just before I turned fourteen.

My father's new orders would take us over three thousand miles from the mainland and friends, his second mandatory "overseas" tour. We could have gone to Belgium or France, but Dad aimed for Hawaii because Uncle Don was stationed there with my aunt. All of us parroted my parents' imposed enthusiasm: *It would be fun! to live in paradise.* Secretly, I was reluctant to say goodbye to my friends and the place I'd carved out in school.

And to our dog.

My father had brought Mitzi home to our Sunnyvale trailer when I was four after he'd come across someone at the grocery store with a box of puppies. I remember her crying at night in the kitchen, where Dad put out newspapers for her accidents. But she grew into a smart, happy dog who was content to keep watch in the backyard and chase squirrels whenever we camped. She resembled an oversized beagle and loved table scraps and car trips. My father had only to jangle his keys and she danced circles around the house, eager to "go for a . . ."

Almost in the same breath as he announced we were moving, my father told us he would be putting our ten-year-old pup to sleep rather than have her endure the isolation of the months-long quarantine required of pets, which would, he said, break her heart.

I accepted the decision as reasonable until the day my dad was scheduled to take Mitzi to the vet to be euthanized and I saw him place her, still alive, in the wooden camp box he intended to use for her burial—"just to see if she'd fit." I watched my dad carry the dog outside, and I followed. I can still see him lowering the frightened animal into the box, which sat on the tailgate of our big blue Chevy Suburban.

I retreated inside when, for the first time in my life, I couldn't control the sound coming from my chest—the guttural, animal wail of grief. When my mother asked what was wrong, I could only point to where my dad was trying to get the dog to lie down in the box.

*   *   *

Hawaii couldn't have been more isolated—or lonesome. On all accounts, my family had entered unfamiliar terrain: a tropical climate whose main features were palm trees, the smell of the Dole pineapple plant, and nineteen varieties of cockroach, coupled with the rage-filled dissolution of my parents' marriage and the combustible energy of honest teenage rebellion. Plus, for the first time in my father's Air Force career, we'd have to live on base. We couldn't afford a house in Oahu's blue-chip market. So we traded our modest split-level home for a small prewar base fourplex crammed in identical rows of buildings across the road from the landing strip on Hickam Air Force Base. Tiny chameleonlike geckos ran along the cinder-block walls of our house. There was a mango tree out back whose fruit stems leaked white fluid that caused skin to erupt in an itchy rash when you touched it. Every time I opened a drawer or turned on a light in a dark room, roaches ran. They fell from the ceilings, landing on my head with soft creepy thuds, or scurried across me at night. The Hawaiian air was thick and wet, and for the first time in my life, summer felt unbearably hot.

Our accommodations were tight—especially at first. For nearly four months after our arrival, my family squeezed itself into a two-bedroom motel room at the Peppertree Apartments, our TLA, temporary living assignment—while we waited for housing. I slept on the couch in the small living room, my brothers in one bedroom, Nancy with my parents in the other. It was strange, beggarly living; we didn't know anyone, and my brothers and I were often shooed outside while Nancy napped. We wandered through the buildings and explored the neighborhood, picking mangoes and trying to climb coconut trees, until someone reported us for truancy—*why weren't we in school?* The move had happened in April, so we'd been allowed to pass before the end of the term. Weren't we lucky, friends and teachers said, to have the long Hawaiian summer stretching out before us? We could learn to surf! We could play at the beach! When the police car pulled up and a wide-bodied officer emerged, I felt a thud in my chest: *Dad is going to kill us.* I looked at Chris, whose already tan body was halfway up the long curve of a coconut tree, and felt the nauseating sensation that I'd done something wrong, along with the white heat of anxiety about what would happen next.

"Hey, *kolohe,* whatcha doin'?" the officer asked my brother.

"We live here," I answered.

He motioned to Chris to come down and took our names and address and marched us home. Once the story had been verified, we were hauled inside.

"What's the matter with you?" Dad's voice was like a slap. He was focused on my brother, the oldest, but we all felt it. The flash of anger that meant anything could happen. After that, we were restricted to the motel room or the metal chairs just outside the door.

The spring and summer days yawned one into the next as we tried to embrace island culture on the most superficial terms, learning how to boogie-board and calling each other "brah." My parents drank mai tais and took us to the beach, where I wore a T-shirt over my bikini because my belly wasn't anything like the bowl-shaped curve of Farrah Fawcett's in the poster my brothers hung in their room. I missed my friends.

Once my family moved into permanent housing, the island— infinitesimal—grew even smaller. The lease on our sand-colored condo came with four pages of rules and regulations: hours when outside lights must be turned on and off, when to run washing machines, what furniture was allowed on the lanai, and curfews by age and rank. The *thunk* of our shouting neighbor hitting his wife and her muffled cries coupled with the overhead roar of planes descending onto the airstrip horrified me. My heart pounded each time a plane boomed onto the runway because I was sure it would crash. In response, I resurrected an old habit of holding my breath when I was afraid, gripping the counter or the soft fabric of the couch, in anticipation of the explosion, the sickening screech of metal as the plane came apart a split second before the house exploded with debris.

My fear of the dark increased. At night, I turned the light switch off and leapt from my bedroom doorway onto my bed, tucking the blankets beneath my feet. I pictured snakes and figures with long clawlike fingers living under the bed. Once shaken awake by my bed rocking side to side, I imagined not an earthquake but something far more sinister and unnatural.

In Hawaii, my father's brutality reached its apex. "Why did you lie *to me*?" he demanded of Chris, who'd fibbed about doing his chores. When Steve got in trouble with a teacher at school, Dad railed, "Don't think you can pull this shit *on me.*" All sins were sins against the father.

But it was me who was hit with a regularity that still registers in my memory as a series of explosions. At each recollection, I am rocked into a strange kind of consciousness with the sting on my face and ears. Most vivid is the time my dad used both his hands to paddle my cheeks back and forth as I counted the swings: four, five, six, seven . . . eight.

We'd quarreled about how to do something and I'd insisted on doing it my way. *You think you're always right,* I'd sneered, and he'd advanced.

Afterward, I glowered—the atomic bomb in a teenager's arsenal—refusing to look away. My lip was swelling. Blood trickled from somewhere between my nose and chin.

"Feel better?" I said coolly. "I know I do."

"You made me do that," he said, turning away.

I was determined to meet his brutishness by being smarter—or at the very least, a smart-ass. Scorn was my weapon and I used it every chance I got, even if it meant I'd get hit again. I opposed him because no one else did. Mine was the defiance of the prisoner before the noose, the panic of a body about to drown.

As my parents' marriage came undone—fueled by my mother's discovery that my father had kept a "boom-boom girl" while he was in Bangkok as part of his Vietnam tour in the sixties—he was at his most intimidating.

Mom and Dad's battles unfolded like matches between two seasoned fighters with completely different strategies, with my father raging and my mother retreating into stony silence, each method meant to draw blood. I once saw my father hurl a vase at my mother while she held my three-year-old sister in her lap. The vase splattered against the wall near my mother's head.

It is one of Nancy's earliest memories.

I don't even remember what the matter was—just my dad threatening and my mother stoic, impassive. When he let the vase fly, she gazed flatly with pale blue eyes.

The atmosphere in the house changed when Dad was in it. Twenty minutes before he arrived home from work—my mother absent, off working at Sears—my brothers and I started a kind of countdown.

"Dad's coming, better pick up your school stuff."

"You better get your chores done," we'd warn in that you'll-be-sorry tone.

Chris and Steve and I rushed around the house putting things away, closing books we were reading, picking up shoes and clothes, cleaning up signs of snacking, trying to erase any evidence of our indolence. In our house, idleness meant laziness, so we scattered like roaches, battening the hatches for the hurricane about to hit.

At 3:20 P.M., Dad walked in swinging. It didn't matter how much we'd done. There was always a reason to yell, to shame.

"What the hell have you been doing?" he'd rage. "Get this place picked up." As quickly as I could I exited to the kitchen, a galley space with a sliding door closure, to start dinner, my newest household job. I'd always helped my dad in the kitchen. He loved to cook while my mother did not. And in there, in the carpeted space adjacent to the only air conditioner in the house, I could find some relief from the heat and my father's temper. On the other side of the door, he barked orders. "Move it or I will make you." "What's the matter with you?" There would be hell to pay.

When my parents weren't fighting, there was the cold menace of silent rage. Fear among my siblings was palpable. My brothers and I retreated to our small worlds. Chris and Steve built models in their room and played Dungeons & Dragons, while I buried myself in books, having graduated from the bodice-ripper romances that populated my junior high years to fantasy novels about otherworldly places filled with dragon riders and ring bearers.

I wrote letters to friends back home using different-colored pens and a manic joking voice full of mock I've-got-this bravado, telling them horror stories about base living, my dad, and my shock that I was now a *haole,* a white girl, a foreigner, while admonishing them "not to worry" because, you know, "Oh well, drama happens." I signed my letters "The Wiz." I think I had been reading Ursula Le Guin's Earthsea Trilogy. I wanted deeply to believe in magic, the ability to transform the world with story and the spell of words.

I spent so much time with books and in my room that I developed a phobia of going outside alone. I put on weight, became so self-conscious that I once burst into tears because the bookmobile was parked on our street and no one wanted to go with me. I couldn't bring myself to walk the block to it alone. My mother, in an uncharacteristic moment, wiped my face and took my hand.

"Come on," she said, and together we walked the two hundred steps as the scent of bougainvillea filled the air.

Still, by the time school began that fall, I'd become so shy and uncomfortable that I went to the library at lunch rather than sit alone in the cafeteria. I simply couldn't face finding someplace to eat away from what I feared would be those who's-she? looks. So, the quiet cool of the stacks with the soft hum of AC and that lovely enforced hush became my sanctuary. And at night, I begged my father to drop me off at the base library after dinner so I could escape the pressure cooker of home.

I took refuge in reading and studied Coleridge and Hawthorne and Truman Capote, reveling in the darkness I saw there. My favorite story, Capote's "The Headless Hawk," featured a painting of a decapitated hawk flying over a headless woman and began with an epigraph from Job: "They are in the terrors of the shadow of death." The protagonist, Vincent, is "a man at sea, fifty miles from shore," who is "never quite in contact" with the world.

Reading Hawthorne, I was equally revolted and hypnotized by Alymer's obsession with his wife Georgiana's birthmark, the husband's need to control his wife, the wife's complicity. Of course I was outraged by Alymer's behavior, but there was a creepiness to their relationship that honestly attracted me. I moved toward the abyss, not really understanding why—feeling its hypnotic pull. I thought my love of Coleridge's woman "wailing for her demon lover" made me mysterious and perhaps profound. I began writing allegorical stories with shadowy figures and turbulent weather, adopting a mantle of darkness that was far bigger—not the superficial Goth darkness of Alice Cooper with bats and black makeup and horror-show lyrics but the soul darkness of a caged animal. There's a school photo of me from one of those years where I am staring down my nose, chin tucked, head cocked in what I'd imagined to be a provocative, model-like pose. My lips are parted slightly and I remember thinking the smoldering air would make me look sexy. Instead, my face is fixed in a sneer; my eyes gaze at the camera with a hate-filled intensity that burns on the page—"I dare you to fuck with me," it says. My transformation from Goody Two-Shoes to glowering teen was more than hormones: I'd forged a dark armor to protect me and keep others at bay.

My sophomore year, I dressed as Quasimodo for the drama club's Famous Movie Icons entry in the homecoming parade, thumbing my nose at beauties like Marilyn Monroe and Blanche DuBois. I thought I was being a rebel, but now I think back to my shambling, fifteen-year-old self with some affection: I was trying to mask a tender heart.

*   *   *

To the outside world, my family appeared happy and well adjusted. In public and at friends' houses, my brothers and I were unfailingly polite and obedient because the consequences had been burned into us by the branding iron of my father's temper. We did as we were told: Get Dad another beer, pick up the paper plates after a beach picnic, watch Nancy. Strangers in the rare restaurant we went to complimented my parents on how well behaved their children were. Family felt like an impenetrable bubble; we tumbled from place to place, bearing our horrible secrets: Dad threatening my older brother, Chris, to "take things out back and settle this like men," and Dad knocking my mother, who was holding my bawling sister in her arms, against the wall when Mom wouldn't put Nancy in her crib. From downstairs, I heard the bump of a body hitting something solid and then my mother's cry, and I lunged up the steps, bellowing in a voice two registers deeper than my own, "Leave her alone!" Adrenaline set a fire in my chest and limbs. I was shaking.

"You asshole, don't you touch her! Don't you touch her!"

I saw the sudden shame on my father's face. Not that he'd done something wrong but that someone had witnessed it.

"Go to your room," he said, not looking at me, as my mother slipped into their bedroom and locked the door.

My father once told me to stop studying in front of the TV as I worked on math homework while watching WWF Championship Wrestling, which featured André the Giant and Hulk Hogan. I loved the drama and the hype, the good guys battling villains. The spectacle made math, my least favorite subject, more bearable, I told him.

"I'm not asking you, I'm telling you."

"I'm fine; it doesn't bother me," I protested.

"If you don't move right now, I will move you," he said.

"Dad!" I objected again.

"Move!"

"Oh, come on!"

"Goddamnit, I said *'MOVE!'*"

My father stood up, lunging at me, but his knee gave out and he crumpled to the floor. I jumped up too, skittering away, but Dad kept coming, dragging himself across the beige linoleum to get to me, his breath coming in piston-like bursts, his head shaking. I grabbed my books and ran—*ran!*—taking the stairs two at a time to my bedroom.

"No one would believe me," my mother said years later. "Everyone thought he was so charming."

And it was true. Anita, a petite southern woman for whom I babysat, once blurted out of the blue, "Oh, your dad's so fun and," she added, "pretty hot stuff!"

I moaned with the typical teen disgust.

"Believe me," she said, nodding her head.

It all came down to a particular brand of masculinity.

"The doc says I have the equipment of a twenty-year-old," my father was fond of saying. Every interaction was a flirtation.

Even with me.

"Fuck you, daughter dear," he'd say in a sugary tone, then pause, "but that would be incest."

Dad admonished me not to scratch "the mosquito bites on my chest" or they'd grow—his answer to the question of puberty. He once announced to a tent full of boys and men when I had my period that the dog shouldn't sleep with me because I was "in heat." Another time, after I confessed giddily and innocently that I had a crush on a boy at school, he told me I'd "better think twice before I lay down on the bed and spread my legs for someone," and then described an erection to me in such aggressive and graphic detail that I was certain I'd never let a guy near me.

It never occurred to me to say one word about any of it.

*   *   *

My mother finally pulled the plug on my parents' marriage just before I turned sixteen. We'd lived in Hawaii for only two years. I imagined Mom remaking herself and living happily and carefree. I was her cheerleader, her confidante, her counsel, cooking up plans for the future.

"You could go back to school!" I said hopefully. "Get a degree and then get a better job!" I said. I urged her to leave my father. I knew I could save her if she'd just *do something*. But she was convinced she was, at thirty-eight, too old to start over. She'd never be anything but a store clerk, she just hoped she could get by.

My brothers and I were given a choice where to live. Chris stayed, perhaps grudgingly; he didn't want to start his senior year at a new school. Steve, who'd managed to linger largely out of the line of fire, remained with my dad out of loyalty and sympathy: no one would be left with him in Hawaii after Chris went to college.

My sister, by then nearly four, and I returned to Colorado to live with Mom, who returned to her former job at JC Penney, where she made four dollars an hour, tops. That and a scant five hundred dollars a month from my father would support us until I turned eighteen. During the divorce hearing, my mom had refused more money, the purchase of a house, and her legal right to part of Dad's Air Force retirement.

"No," she said, when the judge asked her again if she wanted what was rightfully hers. My father had threatened to take Nancy if she'd said yes.

So we moved back to Colorado Springs and I started a new high school my junior year and enrolled in honors and AP courses, a year behind my classmates. For the first time in my life, my friends were solidly middle-class. Many of them owned their own skis and cars, and took vacations to Mexico and Vail. They'd known each other since they'd been in kindergarten.

I worked part-time at a shoe store so I could have clothes for school and help buy groceries. Mom often ate less than my sister and me because there wasn't enough food. The first year and a half, we lived in an apartment. We were poor. But I would leave home before I had to watch, as my sister did, my mother reduced to scheming to provide for her family. Now working at Montgomery Ward, she took credit applications to the flea market, because she got a dollar for each one she collected. If that failed, she would fill them out herself, using information from the phone book.

At first, leaving my father's house was glorious. I remember the smell of Colorado summer rain on the cement pavement—the smell of dirt I so loved—and Dan Fogelberg crooning on the stereo from an album Mom played over and over, "There's a ring around the moon tonight . . ." I saw a few of my old friends. It was good to be home. I was giddy for a few months, flush with strange relief, a swelling sense of euphoria. But then, my mother, who had been my best friend as I counseled her during the divorce, and I began to fight.

"You're just like your father," she said. I was selfish, stubborn.

As my mother doted on Nancy, who she feared would be "damaged" by the divorce, I stayed out more and more with friends, smoking pot and drinking Jack Daniel's. I kept a bottle on the shelf of my bedroom closet, knew which liquor stores would sell it to me.

By the time I was eighteen, I had a habit of rejecting most things out of hand. I didn't like being told what to do. I didn't want to be like any of the people I knew. On the graphed results of a high school career aptitude test, the number of dislikes I had was clear and strong. The left side of the page was populated with dozens of tiny marks corresponding to the things I hated (routine, numbers, problem solving, sales, negotiation, being supervised) and therefore occupations (engineering, business, politics, marketing) that would be unsuitable at best, torturous at worst. The right side was open wide. My highest score? Sixty percent "like" on the possibility of being a Spanish teacher (I had taken French). Clearly, I knew what I didn't like but hadn't the first idea of what I did.

I left home without any idea of where I was going. *No* was the sound of a door slamming shut—it taught me the habit of walking away.

Chapter 3

Marlboro Woman

After I left home, I tested my swagger every chance I got. Proud to be called "fearless" and "tough," I arm-wrestled with guys and downed shots of bourbon with the steeliness of the cowboy hero, once drinking sixteen shots of Wild Turkey at a friend's Thanksgiving "Turkey Trot" by excusing myself at shot twelve to throw up and then returning for the win. It was sheer force of will. I simply would not lose. I'd picked up the art of the bluff from my poker-playing father, and like him, my cool was legendary.

I bulldozed through my undergraduate years at the University of Colorado on my own dime, picking the hardest major I could think of. Oh, I would show the bastards, all right. A premed student, I double-majored in environmental biology and English. I bragged it would make me a better candidate for medical school, after which I'd open my own clinic and deliver babies in a state-of-the-art birthing center while handing out birth control for free.

My smoke-and-mirrors plan dissolved my final year, when on a whim, I studied abroad for a semester. It was the kind of thing, according to my strictly blue-collar father, that rich kids did. I was raised to believe there was a chasm between my life and the lives of people who had money, the corollary of which was that I was to stay put on my side of the economic divide. Certain things— studying abroad, out-of-state colleges, medical school—were not only beyond my reach but, the implication was, supposed to be beyond my ken. Stubbornly, I packed my bags.

In London, the known world opened up and my lens widened. I became an observer, taking down the details of British dialects and slang, astonished at buildings that had been constructed centuries before anything I'd seen in the West, and a countryside tinted in everlasting spring green. I was drunk on place, on discovering that not everyone thought like the people back home. It may have been the thrill of rebellion: I had embraced the forbidden, I'd trampled on one of my father's taboos. But just as true was the fact that a change in landscape forged a change in me. Medical school, I realized with alarm, was a bluff.

What I wanted to be was a writer. More illicit fruit.

"And how will you make money?" my father had demanded of fifteen-year-old me when I declared I would move to the South so I could write stories like Truman Capote. Even then, I knew landscape mattered.

Returning to the States, I fell solidly back to earth, and graduated six months later without a plan. It would take me nearly a decade to screw up the courage to apply to grad school because my father's question loomed: *And then what?* While my brothers dutifully chose careers, got married, and started families, I soloed, living in Boulder—

the liberal town Dad blamed for any of my attitudes or actions he opposed—and held a dozen different job titles as the bottom line beat against my better self. I was a bus driver, summer camp director, after-school-program coordinator, caterer, cook, landscaper, beer vendor, women's clinic assistant, file clerk, storyteller, Girl Scout program director, and for one summer, a Kelly girl. Unwilling to give in to practicality, a torch I had carried since the day I doubled my student loan debt to study abroad, I was always scrambling, changing addresses and living situations as often as I changed jobs.

The woods were the only constant in those years. I camped all over Colorado and in parts of Utah with girlfriends and, at times, alone. Once, settled on a wide bend in the Green River in Stillwater Canyon, Utah, I had watched the sun fall beneath a horizon formed by three distinct geological formations. The passage of thousands of years manifest in the shapes of rocks. My own time line was minuscule by comparison. The thought gave me comfort. To be a speck in a magnificent landscape, to be a part of ceaseless beauty. That night, as I contemplated the deep dome of glitter above, I thought about the Catholic heaven of my childhood. The place of eternal peace. I'd long ago given up the church, and as a little girl, I'd often cried in my bed at night as I tried to imagine forever in a cloud-filled elsewhere populated by ethereal ghosts. It no longer mattered that there would be pearly gates or angels or even god, that kind of perfection had lost its sway. My preference was for the earth, with its rough beauty, its inscrutability, its mixture of shit and muck. "I know what the world is made of, and I still love all of it," says Reyna, the spirited ranch hand Gretel Ehrlich meets in *The Solace of Open Spaces*.

As a slight breeze blew the heat from the day, I dug into the red dirt beneath me. *I could spend eternity here.* Overhead, a shooting star, one of the Perseids, ignited the sky and I lay back, giving my body over to the earth's embrace.

After I was accepted into the creative writing program at CU, I decided to mark the occasion by changing my name. It wasn't a nom de plume I was looking for but an identity, a way of saying, *This is who I am*. In college, I'd learned a ritual of naming myself by my mothers: Karen, daughter of Susan, daughter of Alice, daughter of Mary, daughter of Valborg. Taking Auvinen, my mother's name, would link me to the women who came before; it said they had a hand in forming me too. My father's name—an Italian word that meant big, heavy, thick, just like the man himself—was a weight I'd carried for too long. I knew that naming myself was important—an act of power—but I also knew it was a stone whose splash would ripple across the relationships in my family.

My grandfather Pete was the first to call. "What's the matter? My name isn't good enough for you?" If I changed it, he said, I would be very sorry, and then hung up.

He never spoke to me again.

My father was next. He would support my decision, he said, but then asked that I no longer call him Dad. That privilege had been revoked.

This time I was the one who hung up.

Over the next few days, my father called repeatedly, leaving increasingly threatening messages. He had returned to Colorado after he retired from the Air Force, and in the twelve years since I'd left his house at sixteen, we'd had periods of out-and-out war punctuated by a kind of sticky truce where Dad tried to be my best friend. I'd dodged his temper, but he could still menace. He could still scare me. There was clear fury in his voice after I'd left his messages unanswered and he insisted one last time, he *wasn't asking me but telling me* to call him back, shouting, "You're still my daughter!" I wasn't a person but a possession.

Finally, he threatened to come find me. "I know where you live, I know where you work," he said. He "would not take no for an answer." *We would talk.*

My answer was to quit my job and pitch a tent in the woods. I needed to live cheap and save for school, so leaving ultimately served two purposes: My father would not be able to locate me, and at the end of the summer, the money I saved in rent and utilities would pay my first semester's tuition. I would spend June through August without a phone or an address, telling few people where I was, a place where I'd wake one morning to bear scat just fifty feet from my tent. It would be a decade before my father and I spoke again.

Like Mary Austin's Walking Woman, a woman who walks off her name in the California desert, I faded, even for just a while, into wilderness. Like her, I took my place as an outlier.

*   *   *

At the end of the summer, I moved from James Canyon, three miles below Jamestown, where I'd pitched my tent on a friend's land, to a valley near Bow Mountain in the foothills within shouting distance of the Boulder city limits. I shared the bottom of a house set into a hillside with Dan, a handsome fifty-something who took odd jobs as a handyman and most astonishingly had a string of young, nubile lovers.

There, I watched the green eyes of a mountain lion who hunted across the valley at dusk and hiked up a narrow draw just a quarter mile from my house following a seasonal creek bed. At night, there was no need to draw the blinds. I slept with the windows open and listened for owls, the chirp of crickets the only sound.

Not long after, a dog appeared at my door. He was a part chow, part golden named Aspen, a big feline-looking lug who lived some-where above my house, along the rocky ridge that overlooked the valley, but he adopted me as sure as summer follows spring. I opened the door one glorious morning to find him curled up and fast asleep on the shaded portion of my stone patio near a garden box filled with catmint and marigolds. He leapt up to greet me: his old friend. Charmed, I stroked his woolly apricot-colored fur and rubbed his ears. Aspen had the feral look of a lion, but his disposition was pure lazy cat. He settled in at my feet and fell back asleep.

And became a regular visitor.

Usually I found him stretched out on his side, snoring hoarsely, but sometimes, he'd wander in the open door and back to my room, where I studied. Sometimes, he'd even stay the night. Then, I pretended he belonged to me as I kissed him good night and ruffled his fur. In the morning, I gave him a bit of leftover hamburger. He ate and then sauntered up the hillside and out of sight.

He was like Shane, the angelic cowboy in the George Stevens film, who descends from on high to help the small community, only to leave, ascending back to the mountains in the end. His presence cinched the notion of a dog of my own to my heart. A dog would be the salve to my too often lonely weekends, the answer to the vexation of camping alone. I could go wherever I wanted, companionship guaranteed. The dog would be my pal, my liberator.

So when charming Dan was replaced by a tiny, petulant, and deeply tanned forty-year-old massage therapy student whose disposition was at odds with mine, I decided to trade my valley with a view for a rental farther up the mountain, one that would allow dogs.

"You have to get this house, darling," said my friend Lucia, in her lilting way.

She was reading my cards the way gypsies read—from a playing deck—after I told her about a blue, south-facing Victorian on the outskirts of Gold Hill, a mountain town of two hundred rooted at an elevation of nearly nine thousand feet. It was the only place I'd found that allowed pets. Lucia Berlin was my mentor at CU, where I was finishing my degree in poetry. The cards made a big square on the table in front of me—king of diamonds, ace of clubs, two of hearts.

"You need to get a dog," she said. "You need someone to love." I'm pretty sure she was just pulling my leg, that my cards said something completely different. With Lucia, you could never tell.

The room smelled of cinnamon and apples, from a pot simmering on the stove. We laughed and smoked. By then, Lucia had been on oxygen for a couple of years because scoliosis had collapsed her lung. Whenever I visited, she requested that I bring her "one cigarette, sweetie." Then, we'd sit in her kitchen in a house shoved against the Boulder foothills and, after Lucia turned off her oxygen, lit up. I smoked a clove cigarette to keep her company, a throwback to a habit I'd had for a brief period like everyone else in the eighties. Lucia had a way of making you feel like you were the only one with whom she shared such intimacy and transgression: the forbidden smoke, the jaw-dropping story of Professor X, who'd brought his too young and too drunk girlfriend to a dinner party with the dean.

After she read my cards, Lucia pulled out a picture she'd drawn of a house on a mountainside. On it, she'd written "Karen's home." She placed it on a shelf along the red wall of her kitchen. Then she lit a votive.

"For luck," she said.

Two days later, Doug, of the blue Victorian, called to say I could move in.

Three weeks after I'd unpacked, I brought Elvis home.

Perhaps it was Lucia's magic or maybe her magic was part of the colossal hand of fate that led to moving to a new place, but that dog and I were destined to be together. I'd dropped by the humane society on a whim, dragging my friend Nina, who had a dog of her own. "You're my expert," I told her. In the meeting pen, Elvis circled, peed, and then made a beeline for me. He leaned against my legs and stretched his neck while I stroked his ears. They were like velvet. He had gold, almond-shaped eyes and a black tongue. He was thin, but tall and deep-chested. *He looks easy and sweet,* I thought.

"I think this is the dog," I told Nina, who had short brown hair and big sweet eyes. I couldn't believe it could be that simple.

"Of course, he is," she said. Elvis had been at the humane society for three weeks, but that day was the first day he could be adopted. I put a hold on him and left to buy food and toys and leashes.

It's true what they say—you don't pick the dog, the dog picks you. I went looking for a forty-pound female, a dog who would be obedient and manageable, smart and devoted. A dog like Tikka, my friend Julie's border collie, who waited leashless and quiet for her owner outside stores and restaurants and in the back of Julie's pickup. Instead, I got an underweight fifty-two-pound runner, an escape artist with a mind of his own; he only ever listened to me when he felt like it. With Elvis, I would have to qualify my statements with the phrase *for a husky*—as in "Elvis is pretty well behaved *for a husky.*" He was devoted and manageable. *For a husky.*

The dog had been found loping down a stretch of highway outside Boulder that angled toward cows and open space. He wore a spiked leather collar slung around his neck, a costume at odds with his disposition. Elvis was no brute.

Ignorant of the aggravations that awaited me, I took the handsome, amiably disposed dog home. I remember sitting on the couch watching him sniff the house and then settle on the floor across from me. *What I have done?* I thought. *What if he doesn't like me? What if*

I've made a mistake? The dog didn't like to chew on bones or chase balls. He barely ate. Weeks went by before I could name him. It wasn't at all obvious what he should be called. At first, I thought because of the collar he should be Sid, like the Sex Pistols bassist, but Elvis' disposition was more pretty-boy modern rock than gnashing punk. I tried Ezra and Levi on, but both suggested a roughness the dog lacked. Loki, the name of the Norse god of wiliness and chaos, seemed like asking for trouble. I was already worried he was more dog than I could handle: Impulsive and impatient, he didn't stand so much as stab the ground with his paws. When not sleeping, his body was in constant motion.

Finally, I hit on Elvis. I'd carried a torch for the King of Rock and Roll back in my preteens, when I'd listened to *Aloha from Hawaii via Satellite* until I could sing *and say* the album by heart. Plus, I remembered at the humane society the dog's name tag had said "ARON," Presley's middle name, and I thought I might be shaking my fists at the fates to call him anything but Elvis.

Ass-over-teakettle in love for the first time, I knew I was smitten the day not long after I brought him home when I watched Elvis' paws paddle back and forth while he slept and he called out in a high bubbling cry. Tenderly, I reached out and put my hand on his head, thinking of him alone in his pen at the pound.

"It's okay," I said.

Without a fenced yard, Elvis had to be supervised outside—he simply would not stay near the house, a lesson I learned after a roommate let him out to pee while I was at work and he ran off in a blizzard. When I arrived home, nine hours later, temperatures had dipped into the teens and over a foot of new snow was on the ground. I drove the road circling the town of Gold Hill, head thrust out the window, crying, and calling Elvis' name. I'd had him less than three months. On the fourth trip around, I found him about a mile and a half on the opposite end of the loop from my house just below town, running with four other dogs. Elvis gave that particular high-pitched husky cry as he leapt onto the bench seat of the Toyota pickup truck I drove, as if to say *Where have you been?* Icicles clung like chandelier baubles from his chest and belly. He sidled over to me and put his head on my shoulder, leaning his full weight against me.

*   *   *

A year later, Elvis and I moved to a house on Jim Creek in Jamestown. I was thirty-three, Elvis was two. Unlike the Gold Hill place, which was remote enough that in winter I kept three hundred pounds of sandbags in the back of my pickup and chains on all four wheels during snowstorms in order to make it the last four miles of dirt road to the house, the Ward Street house was thirty yards from pavement.

Elvis and I settled in with my friend Julie, her dog, Tikka, and a visiting professor at CU named Tim. Julie was a landscaper, and together we planted vegetables and flowers in the three gardens overlooking the creek, a stream that churned and roared in spring and whispered beneath ice in winter. Each week, we had family dinner night and took turns cooking the meal.

Our house was situated on the up-canyon end of Jamestown on a sparsely populated dirt road that rambled for miles past a mine and ore-car tracks into the forest. I met a few of Jamestown's characters at the Merc: a man I called *El Patrón*, whose place had one of everything: tipi and hitching post, a fake outhouse with crescent moon vent, rack of antlers over the door, a couple vintage Model A's, white flag for surrender, and a tombstone marking the date of the Sand Creek Massacre; JoJo, who wore the bone from a raccoon penis in his hatband; and Tom Rabbit, a man so blithe, so full of bullshit that when diagnosed with a cancer the doctor said would kill him, he lived. It simply never occurred to him that he could die. He shared a house with Joey, his best friend, and Joey's wife, Suzie, a blowsy woman with hair piled on her head and tired but beautiful crystal-blue eyes, who owned the Merc. On Sundays, the line for her brunch was out the door. Karen Z was the "crazy dog lady" in town. She knew every four-legged by name and temperament but seldom was friends with their owners. We met after Tim reported "my friend" had stopped by, describing Karen, with her barbershop cut and wire-rimmed glasses, standing at the gate collecting kisses from Elvis, and I confessed I didn't know who he was talking about.

"Well, let's invite her to family dinner," said Tim.

Karen rarely cooked herself. The problem was the "one-butt kitchen" in her tiny cabin was buried beneath piles of papers and plates and abandoned bags of groceries. She happily provided the wine for our dinners, so we invited her often.

It would become our morning ritual to walk up Ward Street together with our dogs. I'd arrive at Karen's cabin, nearly the last before the road gave way to forest, with a lidded mug of coffee and Elvis, as Karen's dog, Sophia, woofed and trotted across the one-lane bridge over the creek—Karen's driveway. A black New-foundland mix who was so smart and well behaved I'd nicknamed her St. Sophia, she was the Sheriff to Elvis' Sundance Kid. Her very presence seemed to keep Elvis on trail and in camp more often. On my first camping trip with Elvis, he had buried his food and then mine—I'd turned just in time to see him grab a length of French bread from the table and nose it into the dirt. But when Karen and I backpacked for five days in Grand Gulch and Elvis again scraped dirt and sticks over his bowl, it was Sophia enthusiastically scarf-ing up her dinner that finally coaxed him to eat his own. On that same trip, Elvis wedged himself between me and Karen Z, the third body in a three-person backpacking tent, and stretched himself out luxuriously, humanlike, on his back, while Sophia lay in a perfect black ball, outside.

*   *   *

From the start, Elvis had a keen tricksterly quality. He could appear large and imposing or curl himself into the tightest ball. Once, when we were alone and camping in a deserted corner of Colorado, Elvis raised himself to his full height, guard hairs on his neck standing straight up, as he gave a deep-chested growl toward the lone male backpacker approaching us. He looked as formidable as a wolf. Before that, I'd always joked that he was so nice and loved people so much, he'd give kisses to anyone who tried to break into the house.

He would never be the type of dog who would dutifully trot by my side or come when I called. As soon as he was off leash, he vanished. I'd call, cajole, beg, demand, insist, and even stomp my feet, but the out-of-doors was far too big and enticing a playground. In Grand Gulch, he'd run so much and so hard over the slick red rock that by the third day, he'd run his pads raw.

I'd discovered Elvis' aversion to fenced-in places in Jamestown. Although we had a big yard on the creek, I could not keep the dog in it. He jumped the stone wall into the neighbor's backyard and ran up Ward Street. He weaseled through a ten-inch hole in the chain-link fence, visiting all the houses along Main Street before someone's junkyard German shepherd, a dog who was infamously vicious, chased him all the way home.

Elvis needed exercise, the kind he got only off leash, but his curiosity and flat-out friendliness were too often sources of trouble. I worried constantly that he'd get lost or hurt or simply climb into someone else's car, as he did once when we were visiting my mother in Colorado Springs and he crawled out of the slider window of my pickup, wandering the parking lot of Fargo's Pizza in search of me. When I discovered he was gone, I circled the side streets calling his name, only to return to the lot to see Elvis sitting in the cab of a Ford F-250 as the driver drove around looking for his owner.

On one of our first camping trips to Utah, I let Elvis run ahead of me on a trail in the brand-new Escalante National Monument where there was open grazing. I was perusing the canyon walls for a ruin I kept missing when I realized I hadn't seen my dog for a while. I called for him, answered by the sound of distressed lowing down-trail. *Fuck.* Fearing the worst, I ran. It was a full mile before I found Elvis knee-deep in a muddy pond, where in his enthusiasm to either herd or pursue, he'd broken the skin on the leg of a calf he was pulling. The calf quivered, surrounded by cows, mooing and watching, while Elvis tugged and yanked as if pulling on a chew toy. It was hard to tell what he was doing. He had a sharp predator instinct—I'd seen it kick in time and time again, pulling my dog like a magnet toward things he had no business chasing: deer and elk, moose, bison. As visions of a rancher with a shotgun danced in my head, I leashed Elvis and ran all the way back to the truck.

Something had to be done.

Obedience classes were a bust—Elvis couldn't believe we were spending an hour each week with all those dogs and not playing with them. The bag of yummy treats I carried didn't interest him in the least, and he behaved like a chain-gang prisoner when, as instructed, I put his gentle leader on. The thirty-foot lead I was supposed to hang from his collar and step on when he got too far away on walks whipped up the road trailing my dog, who was out of sight in seconds.

It finally occurred to me that what Elvis needed was an anchor: me. I would be the mooring that kept him from wandering permanently away. So I fastened him to a six-foot leash clipped around my waist: when I stopped, he would learn to stop, when I moved, he did too. We began mornings like this in the house on Ward Street as I made coffee and read the paper, Elvis trailing *me* for a change. Later, I took him for brief walks up Ward Street, stopping occasionally so he'd learn to wait, before letting him run free. The biggest test was the Merc, where Elvis lay at my feet while I drank beer with Karen Z. Suzie allowed dogs inside. At first Elvis wanted to greet everyone, to get up and see what other people and dogs were doing, but I kept him leashed to me, my foot on his lead, his body pinned to the floor.

Eventually, we negotiated a rapprochement. While Elvis would never reliably "come" when called, he responded to "Wait," with a dead stop. He was still out of sight on the trail, but he learned to circle back to check that I was still there.

*   *   *

With Elvis beside me, I picked more and more remote places to camp, searching for spots off dirt roads on Bureau of Land Management land, in Capitol Reef in Utah and on the edge of the Mount Massive Wilderness in Colorado. Campgrounds, where the dog had to be leashed, were a pain. On our first trip, I happily pitched my tent away from the clang and clamor of other campers, only to discover Elvis stayed awake all night himself, alert, head resting on paws as he watched every nocturnal coming and going. At the slightest noise, he sat bolt upright—sleeping next to him was like lying beside the poised body of a rattlesnake. Too often he curled up, only to wake suddenly with a deep and guttural growl that said, *I know you're out there and I'm making myself sound as big and mean as possible.* Jolted to consciousness myself into what was now a weirdly quiet night, I couldn't hear a thing over the boom-boom-booming of my heart, my breath crowding my ears. After he'd sounded his alert, Elvis returned to deep sleep. Not me. I've spent more than a few wakeful nights in the wild, imagining the worst, while Elvis slumbered by my side, legs kicking with doggie dreams, satisfied he'd done his job.

*   *   *

After a few years, I went back to grad school again, this time for a doctorate, trading the mountains for the rolling hills of Wisconsin, humidity, and a truncated horizon for a miserable time. I came back to Jamestown in the summers—once living in a ten-foot trailer near a gulch on Little Jim Creek—because I missed Colorado so achingly. In Wisconsin, city living was one difference—Elvis had to be leashed wherever we went—farmland was another. I couldn't quite find the romance in the dells and moraines, or the hardwood forest, that others did. I felt crowded, claustrophobic. The sky was always obscured, always washed out. I yearned for the clean earth and pine smell of the mountain West, the deep Colorado blue sky, and watching Elvis' tail disappear on the long trail ahead of me.

Taking my exit when I got a fellowship to write my dissertation, I went back to the Jamestown area, moving into a horse barn with no running water, for a year while I wrote.

It was cheap, meagerly living, with a toilet I'd dug myself out back. I bathed with a solar shower hung near the creek in summer and in four inches of warmed water in a stock tank in the kitchen in winter. The place sat on the sunless side of Left Hand Canyon, one canyon over from Jamestown, and the barn, rumored to be a historic Pony Express stop, rested on ten acres, near a pond. Left Hand Creek meandered by.

On the way back to Colorado, I'd taken a route through the Badlands, stopping for a few days. That night, I woke to the sound of piston-like breathing, punctuated by the distinct crunch of ripping grass: *chomp-chomp-whoooooosh* went the sonorous mantra. I'd pitched my tent on a little patch of ground punctuated by half a dozen camp tables with metal awnings. There was no running water, no pit toilet, and no one in sight. Outside the tent in the starry night the biggest buffalo I had ever seen was ten infinitesimally small feet from me, head down, eating a path to my tent flap. I nudged Elvis, who sat up, took one look at the buffalo, and eyed me with a quizzical look—*you got this?*—before he lay back down and resumed snoring. I was afraid that if I startled the animal, he'd trample us, so I started whispering, "Hey, Buffalo, hey there," in a plaintive, quiet voice worlds higher than my speaking voice. I flattened myself against the farthest side of the tent. I think I might have prayed. My heart galloped. After five tense minutes, the animal moved off, casting a shadow the size of a VW against blue nylon. Later, I woke again to the whole tent shaking: The buffalo had returned to scratch himself against the metal awning nearby.

Now he was just playing with me.

In the morning, I pocketed the buffalo fur he'd left on the awning and walked Elvis the half mile to the creek for a bath with Dr. Bronner's peppermint soap after he'd rolled in the pile of fresh bison scat. Later that fall, after I moved into the Bar-K cabin, I tied the fur with a piece of red embroidery floss and hung it from a hoop strung with rabbit fur. On the skin side of the hoop, I drew lightning bolts with charcoal. I'd heard a story that lightning was the energetic proof of the union of earth and sky, and that the earth was healed wherever it was touched in this way. I had always liked the idea of dramatic transformations—that your life could change in an instant—but never imagined how its resulting shock and collapse might feel.

There's a story about Rabbit calling her fear to her. She sees a coyote playing in the field and shouts, "Coyote, I am not afraid of you." When the coyote ignores her, she gets louder and louder until she's jumping up and down on a rock crying to the heavens, "Coyote, Coyote!" Only then does the coyote look up, bound over, and pounce. "Let me not be afraid" was my prayer, and camping and living alone was my shout-out to Coyote. That day, as I tied the fur to the hoop, I thought the buffalo had been reminding me that my tendency to imagine the worst could get in the way. I made the hoop as a shield against all the unseen, unnamed things that scared me.

It would burn along with the rest of my things.

PART II

Refuge

Chapter 4

Summer into Fall

I n the days after I'd watched my house burn, a great weight lifted. I felt strangely euphoric, no longer saddled with counting every penny for rent or bills, unburdened by a house full of goods that required care, cleaning, or mending. Mine was the ecstasy of the unencumbered. There was a moment of pure, birdlike flight as I soared above it all, followed by the heft of gravity, a slow recognition that all evidence of my existence had been reduced to ash. There was nothing left to mark the way I'd come. No books, no papers; no writing, no words. Not one diploma. I could disappear without a trace.

This is what dying feels like, I thought. In the end, it would be so easy to let go.

I was flying in air.

I did not yet know I was in free fall.

* * *

My carefully constructed fantasy of self-sufficiency popped like a balloon. I was startled to suddenly *need* so much. In a world where

I'd have to begin all over again, I could no longer rely solely on grit and determination; I would also require help. Red-faced at the thought, I balked. It's our resistance that kills us, but resist I did, and that made the going so much rougher.

What might have happened if I had lived in a bigger town like Boulder, a place where my inclination to be anonymous would have allowed me to fall quietly through the cracks? In Jamestown, help swirled around me. The community arrived like the cavalry. Nancy E, a woman with whom I'd bonded over a passion for food and Fiesta ware, took me on two shopping sprees to Target, where just the basics like underwear, a few clothes, and toiletries added up to more than half a month's rent. My friend Kelly, a former student, passed a hat among her coworkers at the salon where she cut my hair and together with Karen Z procured leashes and bowls, medicines and toys, and a new dog bed for Elvis. Even Joey, my cantankerous boss at the Merc, whose tight-lipped midwestern sensibility too often clashed with my direct nature, put a donation jar with my name on it on the bar. We'd had an uneasy alliance ever since he'd taken over the café from Suzie, who'd hired me and then left for a warmer life in Mexico. Word went out and postal customers along my rural route left money in envelopes in their boxes. More donations arrived in the mail. Anonymous checks. Care packages of bedding and clothes. Marshaled in part by my good Wisconsin friend Oody, colleagues and professors worked to replace some of the books on my doctoral list, loading them into boxes along with pens and notebooks. The town held a benefit.

Jamestown, like a lot of mountain towns, was a strange brew of aging sixties idealists, young hippie-wannabes, folks who wanted to be left alone or, like me, were cranky around too many people, along with some red-blooded libertarians. Into this cocktail went a handful of hard-core stoners, alcoholics, and people needing to be medicated, a group that crossed all lines and demographics. I'd developed a kind of love-hate relationship with the community, my stance alternating between bemused and disapproving outsider. When I wasn't working at the Merc, I let my truck slow at the dip in front and simply waved at the crowd of regulars, which always included Rabbit, his string-thin gray ponytail snaking down his back, along with any number of mountain bachelors you could count on to be sipping beer or smoking cigarettes year-round outside. So when these same folks, some about whom I'd formed strong opinions or flat-out disliked, showed up to bid on items and buy beer, I roasted on the twin spits of chagrin and embarrassment.

At the benefit, the town drunks orbited a keg outside the town hall, one of a handful of buildings dating back to the early 1900s. They filled their red party cups, probably unaware that their dollars would pay for a couch, a dinner table, and a bed. Inside the hall, a band called the Unknown Americans played so enthusiastically and loud, the crowd hovered outside, bunched around a fire in a fifty-gallon drum. The day was spring wet and cold.

Karen Z, who only ever wore jeans and flannel and men's Beefy-Ts, worked the crowd outside like a carnival barker, selling peekaboo shots of a photo of her twenty-year-old self as a Catholic novice for five dollars a pop. Others bid on donated items or stuffed cash into a jar. People filled plates with potluck dishes and chatted with each other.

I left Elvis in my truck and tried to drink the beer that was handed to me. I wish I could say I took it all in effortlessly, but the truth is I haunted the periphery of the party, more uneasy with condolences and well wishes than I would have been with condemnation and blame. Kindness was a spotlight that branded me as pitiful.

When my father, informed by a panicked message from my sister, had called the morning after the fire to offer money, I was still in shock, and his "I love you" caught me off guard. I sobbed, "I love you too." We'd seen each other when my grandfather died a few years back. That had been our only contact in a decade. The thick mud of discomfort ran down my limbs: I was in no mood for a hasty reconciliation—the price of accepting my father's aid. *But I needed help.* Dad said he would send a check.

Days later, I fled to Moab.

There wasn't much to load in my truck, a Therm-a-Rest, sleeping bag, a one-burner propane stove, and a French-press travel mug. All new, all purchased at the last minute. The tent and cook stuff was Karen's.

Elvis riding shotgun, I aimed my 4Runner west toward a campsite along the Colorado River near Castle Valley, a place I'd camped dozens of times. The spot was private, tucked behind a small butte overlooking a bend in the river, with a view of the wide hand of the valley and its sandstone towers and bluffs.

Once there, my ritual was to gather light. In the morning, I'd watch the cliffs above the river flame red, the line of sunrise washing down the rocks as I tried to memorize the precise color while Elvis chased chipmunks between sage and rabbitbrush. At the end of the day, after a hike with the dog, after lazing in the sun near the creek up Courthouse Wash, I would return to camp, turn my chair around, and take in the whole process in reverse: the shadow of sunset crawling up the spires of Fisher Towers, the landscape deepening to the color of blood. Tracking the changing landscape made me pause. The chatter in my brain dulled to a whisper, my pulse slowed. I took a few deep breaths.

By the time the highway dropped down to the Colorado River Valley, it was almost 5:00 P.M. and the light flashed against the rocks. Relief flooded my chest as I anticipated settling in. But a No Camping sign blocked the turnoff. What had been a vague dirt road that looked like it moseyed to nowhere was now a distinct path clearly blocked by a sign emblazoned with a red-slashed tent.

I panicked. By now I'd expected to be sipping the Crazy Ed's chili beer Karen Z had put in the Playmate she loaned me, waiting for the sun to set, but I had gotten a late start. Backing up, I turned my truck north and raced through a series of alternate campsites I knew from years of exploring the valley. Each one off the beaten path, away from campgrounds and people. Every single site was inscribed with the same sign. Desperate, I drove up Castle Valley and into Fisher Towers to check the campgrounds there: too many people. And Elvis would have to be on a leash, which meant we'd both be miserable.

Two hours later, the sun had long since slid behind the river-side wall and the valley was dusted in blue. It would be dark soon. I had to make a decision: go to a campground where bands of cyclists and noisy RVs stood between me and a quiet night or poach a campsite.

After nearly three weeks of sleeping in half a dozen different beds and wearing hastily purchased or donated shoes and clothes, I yearned for familiarity, a place where my history was written in the pattern of sage, the curve of a vermilion butte. So I nosed my 4Runner past the sign, checking my rearview mirror the whole way, heart pounding. *What if someone saw?*

At the campsite, I kept Elvis close. Too nervous to make a fire or a hot dinner, I wrote by the light of a headlamp held in my hand and ate cheese and crackers. The river, full of red silt, whirled darkly by. Elvis sat on the edge of the camp, looking out.

Ghost rain fell in the distance. I watched the clouds bend toward the horizon, spilling rain that would evaporate before it reached land. I'd lost everything so suddenly and so unexpectedly that the pieces existed now only as vague memories, as rain that does not touch the earth, a presence haunting the horizon. Still, I was unable to mourn. I knew I was not my stuff. That fact was clear to me the moment I saw the fire. It felt silly, childish, to grieve objects. I had Elvis. I was alive. I wouldn't let myself wallow in disappointment. *What good would that do?*

But a persistent emptiness filled me, a feeling of great space and remoteness, as if I'd been hollowed out too. I was holding my breath, waiting for the next terrible thing. In the months that followed, I became a somnambulist as I refused heartbreak—refused feeling anything at all—and put my shoulder against the rock of rebuilding.

I spent a fitful night in the back of my truck, keys hanging at the ready from the ignition, because I was afraid to pitch the tent and woke at the sound of each car, each appearance of headlights upriver.

In the morning, I loaded my truck and went into Moab, where the sidewalks were loaded with people wearing mountain biking baggies and gloves. After southwestern eggs Benedict at my favorite breakfast spot, I headed out of town.

The surrounding area was just as overrun. People rode, hiked, choppered, and flew. Moab had been a destination for well over two decades and the annual crowds had multiplied accordingly, but this year seemed far worse. I drove down one deserted dirt road—hopeful, in search of a campsite—only to have a paraglider land a hundred feet in front of me. She waved sheepishly, as I waited for her to gather her chute.

That day, I found a spot in Potash tucked between the canyon wall and a small trickle of a stream, but by midday, the late March sun was so unseasonably hot that Elvis hid, panting, beneath the truck and I packed again. I found another campsite north of Moab, on the mesa that led to Dead Horse Point. The sun slanted behind a massive butte, and I set up camp next to it. The next morning, I woke to a Jeep with oversize tires trying to crawl up the sandstone face not fifteen feet from my tent. It was 6:00 A.M.

"I want to go up there," said a baseball-capped man, pointing to the rock behind me. "I've been driving all night to get here."

I stood my ground, but after a morning of listening to the high grinding hum of ATVs on a loop nearby, I broke camp again.

Although I was about to be forty, I felt the same as I had so many times growing up. I'd been struggling for years to dig in, but I kept circling, trading jobs for grad school, one rental for another, reenacting my itinerant childhood. I was the furthest from settled I'd ever been. I wanted a home, but I wanted landscape too. A place that belonged to me. *Hadn't that been why I'd moved farther and farther into the mountains?* We seemed to fit. Now, I doubted everything. Placelessness was a grief deeper than all that had happened.

I spent a final night in Kane Creek. It was home to a spectacular campsite marked by an ornate hand-built terrace fashioned from sandstone and river rocks featuring a bench circling a fire pit and rock chairs in the creek. Campers had added to it over the years until it was a small oasis out on the plain. Karen Z and I had camped there once, but now I couldn't find it. I drove down the wide valley only to discover more engine-gunning ATVs, tires kicking up clouds of dust. I was restless. Agitated. Nothing felt right.

So I headed home to Colorado, all too aware there was *no home* to return to. I thought suddenly of the morning I'd woken on a foam pad wedged between a love seat and the entryway to the kitchen in Karen Z's Jamestown cabin. My former neighbor and friend's home on the banks of Jim Creek was claustrophobic, the space crammed with boxes of camping gear and forgotten bags of who knows what, newspapers and magazines, cat beds, and stacks of books. More wet spring snow was falling as I dug through a sack of hastily donated clothes for something warm and pulled on the only sweatshirt that fit me. *It smelled like someone else.* Something gave way in me, the same way shards of sandstone give way in the desert. I heard myself whimper. *Hah-ha-ha-ha,* I cried.

On the way out of town, I stopped at the put-in at Ida Gulch near what had been my favorite campsite and watched the ruddy hues of the Colorado swirl by. The sky was overcast; there was no sun today. Coming here had always made me feel rooted. Not this time. I took out a rose quartz heart a friend had given me after the fire—*for healing,* she'd said.

I threw it in the river.

* * *

Karen Z didn't share my reticence when it came to asking for help, and by the time I had returned, she'd unabashedly procured the use of a vacation cabin in Peaceful Valley, a dozen miles northwest of Jamestown along a two-mile stretch of the St. Vrain River, where I could stay for free until I found another rental. It was owned by a couple about my parents' age who had a handyman business and lived across the street.

I arrived with three garbage bags filled with everything I now owned in the world, along with a laptop on loan. Waldy, a short man with bushy eyebrows and a beard, armed with a powerful hug, called ebulliently from across the street. "Come to dinner!"

I resisted. But then Elvis went over to greet him, prancing around patches of snow, bowing to play with his massive dog, Juno, a part Great Dane, part Newfoundland who looked like a big black tank on long spindly legs.

Waldy had once cooked at the Merc, when Suzie owned it. When I first moved to Jamestown, I remember seeing him with a cigarette dangling from his lips as he flipped hash browns and pancakes on the flattop in the morning. His specialty at home was Polish food. That night, we ate soup with mushrooms and cream and dill, and then sausages and lots of red wine. His wife, Kara, had sharp hawk-like features and long black hair. She did healing and bodywork and offered a free massage whenever I wanted. Our conversation was effortless and funny, and for the first time in a while, I laughed and laughed. Sitting at their table, Elvis asleep at my feet, I could see that we would become good friends. And yet, I felt like a bug on a boiler plate: The words *thank you* seemed ridiculously inadequate.

*   *   *

The semester ended and my birthday loomed. For months, I'd anticipated being triumphant at arriving at a milestone *and* a hopeful new chapter in my life, but now gloom obscured my delight. I was stepping off into the unknown but I was unprovisioned. What's more, the path I'd cut had been sheared: I'd be starting from the beginning.

All too aware of the difference between where I thought I'd be and where I was, I fled to Taos to celebrate alone. On the day of my birthday, I visited the D. H. Lawrence Ranch and the sunflower-adorned chapel where Lawrence's ashes were entombed in a silver-painted cement block, inscribed with his initials; a phoenix—Lawrence's personal symbol—was inset in the wall above. "Are you willing to be sponged out, erased, cancelled, / made nothing?" he wrote in a poem about the mythic bird. I rubbed his initials into my notebook and took a photo of Lawrence in his final resting place.

That night, I ate dinner at an elegant restaurant on the plaza, where I asked the waiter, Alessandro, a handsome Greek man with shoulder-length curly hair and twinkly brown eyes, to pair a glass of wine with each course. The restaurant was empty and we talked about the fire and placelessness. He'd come to the United States with just a backpack. He had no family.

At the end of the evening, Alessandro said he'd like to bring a special bottle of wine to my casita after work. *Okay,* I said, but as he walked away, I panicked. *Was he flirting or did he feel sorry for me, alone on my fortieth birthday in a strange town?*

I hadn't had a boyfriend since my undergraduate days. Except for a drunken fling in Wisconsin with a poet I'd misjudged as romantic and misunderstood, I'd not been touched in years. I hadn't the first idea of what Greek Man wanted. Conversation? Kinship? Birthday sex? In the end, I rethought having a strange man come to the lone house on the Mesa where I was staying. No one knew where I was.

As I paid the bill, I told him I'd decided against a nightcap.

He smiled graciously as I tried to read either disappointment or relief in his face.

* * *

That year, the mountain spring was wet and the early summer wetter. In July, I signed a lease on a cabin where the grass was already hip high among aspen trees and ponderosa. I'd seen it on my mail route, tucked into the center of a dirt road that looped away from the main drive between Jamestown and the Peak to Peak Highway. It was tiny and a bit dumpy, hidden behind rock outcroppings, stowed among aspens on an acre of land bordered by empty lots on two sides.

At first I'd said no.

Sitting at the same elevation as my Bar-K place and just a few miles across the mountaintop, this cabin wasn't insulated in any modern sense. Made of thick wood two-by-fours, it had once been a summer fishing cabin and was built for the warmth of July and August, when just a plywood floor and single-pane windows would do. The current owner had bought it when mountain housing prices were still low and, along with her boyfriend, an amateur carpenter, converted the eighteen-by-twenty-eight-foot shack on pylons to a year-round cabin with plumbing and a bedroom. A rock wall went up around the piers that held the cabin off the ground, and rigid foam insulation sheets were nailed beneath the floor. A well was dug. Untrimmed drywall separated the kitchen from a bathroom and the bedroom from an alcove that could be used as an office. A coal stove salvaged from an inn just outside of Leadville had been hauled in and placed on a hand-built sandstone hearth. A couple of inefficient electric heaters—backup—were shoved into the living room, where one wall bowed out like the hull of a ship under the massive weight of roof beams four times too big. The flat bottom of a wooden ammo box had been nailed to the wall above the stove, and a limbed pine tree seemed to support the south wall where the kitchen and dining areas met. Some of the cabinets lacked proper shelves. The cabin had the feel of someone's neighborhood clubhouse—proudly put together with a collection of cast-off parts and reclaimed material. Cracks of light seeped between the two-by-fours into the dark interior space and the windows *recessed in,* the sills located on the outside of the cabin walls.

I was wary of renting another home heated by wood and worried about the state of the probably-not-up-to-code wiring, not to mention the age of the stove. But in the end, driven by economic need—it was the only affordable place on the mountain—I took it.

Neighbors were seasonal or scarce, and that suited me. I just wanted to be left alone. In the summer, the cabin was hidden behind its own curtain of green; I could walk around naked and no one would ever know.

To the east, Overland Mountain lay a short walk through national forest land past a pond. From there I could see both the Colorado plains and the edge of the Continental Divide. To the west from the deck, I glimpsed a bit of the Indian Peaks, so named because they are said to resemble a reclining Indian and his horse.

For Elvis, the place was paradise. I tried only once to put him in the half-acre dog run, but after he barked his displeasure for a full hour, I gave up. Instead I got in the habit of simply letting him out the door to peruse the yard, sniffing for evidence of critters—rabbit and ground squirrel; chipmunks and coyote. Eventually, he'd wander down the driveway, nosing his way around part of the looped road to the drives of two neighbors whose homes were hidden from sight, as if it was his *job* to inspect them. Then he'd bound back through pine and wildflowers, taking the stairs two at a time, circle, and plunk down at their edge on the top of the deck and watch the yard. The cabin was off the main road, so I didn't need to worry about cars, and when Elvis wanted in, he simply barked once at the door.

After so many years of tracking him down when he escaped a fenced yard, or having to leash him whenever we went outside, it was a relief not to have to constantly look over my shoulder, wondering where my dog was. And Elvis was happy with his new freedom. *Maybe he's more mature now,* I thought of my eight-year-old dog. Or maybe, like me, he simply needed space in order to stop running away.

*   *   *

Just a few weeks after I moved in, I woke to the sound of empty metal cans clanging in the dirt, and I hastily threw on a sundress and rushed outside, leaving Elvis sleeping on his bed. Low clouds dredged the mountaintop, and the Indian ricegrass was tall from long days of rain. The summer continued to be cool. There was only mist and the damp smell of earth. I picked up trash scattered in the yard and was putting it back in the can for which my landlord had promised to build a shed when I noticed a wide expanse of flattened grass that led into the mist. I spied an open trash bag behind the shed about halfway between me and the road, and went to retrieve it when I heard the unmistakable *shush-shush-shush* of something moving along the berm.

"Hey, Bear," I called, quietly. I grabbed the bag and picked up the trash, all the while talking to the bruin. When I stood upright, the unseen mammal gave two quick chuffs of air from its mouth. A warning. It was closer than I thought. The grass shushed again, and before I could think it might be moving toward me, I heard its loud gallop on the road retreating into the morning mist.

*   *   *

When the college library contacted me to see if I still wanted my copy of Terry Tempest Williams' *Refuge* held on reserve, I was jubilant: *One of my books had survived!* Like any book lover, I could pick a volume from my library and tell you the story of not only where I was but *who* I was when I first read it. Books keep our histories. When I'd read *Refuge,* a memoir that chronicles Williams' mother's cancer along with the flooding of the Great Salt Lake, and celebrates the bond between women and nature, mothers and daughters, I was so moved I called my own mother. We'd grown apart since I'd left home, our relationship a sticky combination of unrealistic expectations and disheartening disappointments. I wanted a mother who was assertive and openly proud: My mother wanted a daughter who didn't demand so much. Inspired by Williams' emotional guts, I'd picked up the phone.

"Nothing else matters," I said. "You're my mother and I love you."

Just a few months after the library called, Williams came to Boulder to receive the Wallace Stegner Award at CU. It was early fall. The mountain smelled like woodsmoke and the summer grasses had been flattened by the first frost. At the feeders—the return of winter birds: junco and chickadee.

"You have to go," Karen Z said. "You have to tell her what happened." *It was a sign,* according to her, the woman who never said such things.

"She won't care," I said, adopting indifference.

I know now that stoicism is a stance whose backbone is fear, but at the time I was haunted by the feeling that somehow I'd deserved exactly what I'd gotten. I pretended to Karen that the resurrection of Williams' book and her appearance were simple coincidence, while hoping that some kind of magic was afoot. I have always tried to believe in a mystical world, despite the mule kicks it had leveled at me. I didn't know what Williams could possibly say to me, but I knew it was important to tell her my story.

"Memory," she wrote in her memoir, "is the only way home."

The university ballroom was packed on what was one of those glorious fall evenings on the Front Range: blue skies fading to a dusk that didn't yet require a winter coat. I'd seen Williams speak before, but this time, she was tentative, as if translating from a different language: She had just returned from Rwanda.

"I still have one foot in that country. I still have no words for what I saw." Her experience with darkness and terror forced a new perspective, she said. It was important "to be a witness, to explore the underbelly."

I thought about Lawrence's poem: "Are you willing to be dipped . . . into oblivion?"

"This way," said Williams, "that hole in our hearts becomes an opening."

Afterward, I stood for almost an hour, as Williams spoke warmly to every single person in line. When it was my turn, I thanked her and handed her my book before telling her how it was one of a handful of things that survived a fire. To my embarrassment, my voice cracked.

She nodded her head. "You are brave," she said, looking me in the eye.

I shook my head. "No."

It had nothing to do with guts. *You just keep going.* I had a choice to put one foot in front of the other—or die. Only once did I think about stopping, and then I thought of Elvis—*who would care for such a pain-in-the-ass dog?*

I could not open the book until I got home. When I did, I read: "For you, Karen: To the growth of transformation and restoration, with Love, TTW." In the months ahead, when all else seemed dark, those words were a bit of light: Renewal *was* possible.

Chapter 5

Winter

U p on the mountain, summer was easy: The temperature at 8,500 feet rarely rose above eighty-five and the world was green and glorious. Aspens clacked in the breeze and hummingbirds whirred across meadows gone crazy with wildflowers. Mornings dawned open and wide blue, but by noon, the sky blackened and thunder rumbled, hail ricocheting in tall grasses in the yard and bouncing off the uneven sandstone-brick path. But summer lasted only about fifteen weeks. The rest of the time, the mountain belonged to winter, crowding fall and spring with the promise of snow.

I shouldn't have been surprised that winter came early to the High Lake cabin and the mountain transformed overnight. I'd watched all through September as the summer grasses browned along the berm where the skeletons of spiky Russian thistle grew as tall as children and the bowl of aspen trees surrounding the cabin ignited one by one with gold fire—both hiding the cabin from view. Now in mid-October, as unadorned branches stretched toward the cloud-filled sky and the grasses lay flattened beneath two feet of snow, my cabin was suddenly visible from the road. Without the camouflage of summer, I felt exposed.

Drifts buried the deck and made high walls on the railings; the steps down to the yard were mere indentations. I hadn't even hauled up the wood box from its summer home near the dog run, and my woodpiles were buried. One cord of pine lay neatly stacked in tidy protected rows against the shed, but the bulk of my best-burning wood—two full cords of irregularly chunked oak railroad ties— had been dumped in a twelve-by-six pile in the yard and lay hidden beneath a tarp. Before the storm, the pile measured five feet at its peak, but now it was larger—a mountain, the slopes merging with the berm where I'd seen the bear.

Winter was another country.

From the bottom of the deck, I hastily dug paths to both wood-piles by carving out a trail straight left to the pine before backtrack-ing to make a Y that veered toward the oak. Then I filled a postal delivery crate, a leftover from the rural route job I'd recently quit, with mostly pine and some small pieces of oak I excavated from one edge of the mound. I was beginning to see the work I'd created for myself by keeping the oak out in the open, but there was no place else for it and nothing I could do now anyway. I would be digging out blocks all winter.

Too soon, I'd learn that the berm provided not protection, as I'd thought, but an excellent ski-jump-like ledge for the winter wind. By January, the oak pile would shape-shift and become part of the landscape, disappearing beneath drifts and a crust of frozen snow so thick, my twice-weekly routine would be to punch through it and shovel off slabs of snow in order to yank up the tarp and expose a new section of wood. It was like trying to remove snow from the bottom of a mountain by pushing it upward. Inevitably, I found myself standing on top of the pile, digging frozen blocks out from a hole I'd created in the snow, a bit like ice fishing. It would take me a couple of winters to figure out I could lessen my labor by installing a snow fence, using larger overlapping tarps, and marking the edges of the woodpile with green survey stakes.

Elvis leapt over and through the sides of the paths I shoveled—now more than knee deep—tail fanning out behind him. His face drawn back in what can only be described as a grin, he made chuffing sounds as he pounced and buried his muzzle all the way to the ears to sniff for mice beneath the snow. His tracks zigged and zagged and circled the yard; he was a hotshot skier in fresh powder. I laughed out loud. In all the world there is nothing as happy as a husky in snow.

I looked across the yard, whose edges were softened like the bodies of voluptuous women. Smoke drifted from the cabin's chimney. The air held the hush of winter. Peace and quiet, at last.

At first, it seemed fitting to begin the winter in this state of mind, to embrace the quiet days and long nights, and rebuild, suspended in its embrace. Like the subject of Wallace Stevens' poem "The Snow Man," I would cultivate "a mind of winter" up there on the mountain. I would surrender to the season, learn to love the presence in emptiness, "the nothing that is." Isolation would be my salvation: It would be just me and landscape.

But winter was a two-edged sword. Living in that kind of imposed isolation required a delicate balance, one I was nowhere near achieving. What I thought was emptiness was simply absence. I was running away, not to.

My everyday life was the opposite of nothing. I juggled jobs cooking, teaching, and freelancing, and larded my spare time with tasks: load the firewood box, chop tinder, bury ash, feed the fire, shovel snow, walk and feed the dog, cook.

I avoided writing. Whole months had passed since the fire without a single entry in my journal. I couldn't even muster simple notes about the day; even that was too much gravity. Instead, I kept busy. I just wanted to put as many miles between me and the previous spring as possible.

Too much had happened and was going to happen—and each time, the shock was the same as an avalanche on a blue-sky day: the simultaneous rumble and impact; snow, lingering, on the horizon.

*　　*　　*

I hadn't seen my teacher Lucia Berlin for three years when I heard she slipped away peacefully in her sleep on her sixty-eighth birthday in November, a book in her hands. Even though I knew she had cancer, the news took the air from my body. *Too soon*. It was an end that seemed in some ways too placid for Lucia—a woman whose life was like a beautiful blowsy brawl. Yet it smacked of a quiet dignity that would have pleased her immensely.

We'd grown apart since she'd left Boulder for California while I was busy with my doctorate, the failing entirely mine. I wanted Lucia to adore me, to lavish me with immense praise the way she did with other students. But she was hard on me and my work, and I was never sure why. So I put some miles between us, convincing myself that our closeness in Boulder—all those hours indulging in cigarettes and gossip, the dinner parties and lunches—was the stuff of smoke and mirrors, that her generosity was too good to be true. When I heard about the circumstances of her death, living in a son's converted garage, her description of radiation—"like having your bones ground to dust"—I wailed. *Oh, Lucia.*

Suddenly I thought of the beautiful Manzoni bowl that had belonged to her. I'd long admired a similar one when I worked at a kitchen store in Boulder in grad school, but the bowl was ridiculously expensive, beyond my reach. Lucia had a small version filled with fruit sitting on her kitchen table. Her tiny rental flat was populated with eloquent pieces of beauty—*preciosos*—even as she struggled to make ends meet. She'd told me the story of how she'd ordered the bowl from a catalog, in celebration of her new job at the university. Only after it arrived did she realize her mistake: The bowl she'd paid so much for was the smallest of three sizes.

"I supposed for that price I was getting the biggest bowl," she said with a laugh, as she waved her hand in the air above it. "Well, I thought, I better use it every day."

As I ran my fingers over the smooth red and gold and blue bands, I teased, "When you die can I have this?"

She'd handed it to me just before I left Boulder for my Ph.D. in the Midwest, along with a note: "For your Wisconsin dinner parties, Darling. Love L." I'd last seen it filled with lemons when I left the Bar-K cabin in March.

At Lucia's memorial my friend Elizabeth, another of Lucia's students, who'd flown in from Rome to attend, handed me a book from Lucia's library. Chekhov. Her favorite. Lucia had often spoken of his stories as "perfect, unadorned, true." And I'd hated them. They were subterranean in their turmoil and subtlety was not an art to which I aspired. I could hear Lucia giggling.

Inside Elizabeth had tucked a photo of the three of us at breakfast—each sporting a different shade of auburn hair. Another life. *Precioso.*

*   *   *

As winter thickened, so did my grief. But it was silent and plodding. I retreated to my cabin, pulling down the prayer shawls tacked above the windows at night. I saw little of my friends. I tended the fire and watched movies and walked Elvis and stewed pot roast and cacciatore in a big enameled cast-iron Dutch oven, eating artfully prepared meals alone by candlelight. By the holidays, I was avoiding everyone, making excuses. In December, Kelly, who along with her dog, Maasai, hiked with Elvis and me a few times through the brittle fall, offered to share her hotel room if I came down to Denver to celebrate her birthday the week before

Christmas, but I shrugged her off. I wanted to disappear into the crystalline air.

Snow fell on Christmas Eve, fat flakes filling the sky. I'd strung white lights in the aspens off the deck and inside put more on the tree trunk against the south wall. The next morning the sky was achingly blue as drifts of snow sparkled in the sun. I listened to Mozart's Requiem and made lemon soufflé pancakes and maple sausage. The ritual of food was my celebration.

Karen Z stopped by with her dog, Sandy, the twelve- or fourteen-year-old golden she'd rescued six months after Sophia died because she'd been told the dog's age and condition made her unadoptable. That had been nearly four years ago. Sandy followed me into the kitchen, eager as she always was to see what delicious thing might fall on the floor: She didn't act like an old dog. Karen produced a new chew toy, an octopus with eight squeakers, for Elvis. He shook it and pranced around the room, head tucked like a circus horse, showing off. Together, Karen and I walked the quiet roads circling the mountaintop with the dogs, the crunch of fresh snow beneath our boots, the smell of pine smoke in the air. Back at the cabin, we warmed up with a good small-batch bourbon slipped into coffee before Karen loaded Sandy and headed for work. Later in the day, Elvis and I would feast on garlic-laced rib roast and mashed potatoes, along with a bordelaise sauce I'd spent over an hour and a twenty-dollar bottle of cabernet making. Wind blew the new snow across the meadow, exposing the tops of dried summer grass.

The next day I woke to news of the Indian Ocean tsunami and emailed Kelly, who by then had been in Sri Lanka for exactly two days, enjoying her unofficial honeymoon in a cabana on the beach. I was sure she "was okay," I wrote in the email, "just checking in." *Be safe,* I signed, *Love.*

Two days later, when I opened the newspaper in the early light of a cold morning as Elvis did his tour of the neighborhood, Kelly was on the front page.

The same sound that emerged from my body when I saw the fire, when I heard about Lucia, rose now. I stumbled back to the cabin, howling.

Impossible. Kelly, who'd had wild curly hair, who said things like "Yeah—I gave him a cup of kick-ass." She'd traveled from Asia to South America alone and put herself through school working as a cosmetologist. At thirty-five, she was about to finish a degree at CU she'd begun years before as my student at the community college. *It would take a tsunami,* I thought.

Hadn't I just seen her? She'd cut my hair and we'd talked about her "official" wedding in Paris the following year. She'd met Nassir in Guatemala, and after a year of meeting in places like Madagascar and South America, they had secretly married in Nassir's village in Afghanistan last summer. No one but a few close friends knew.

"You're coming to Paris," she'd said flatly. "Elvis will be fine." She knew I had been reluctant to leave my dog ever since he developed a nearly fatal autoimmune disease two weeks after I'd returned from a monthlong residency while living in Wisconsin and his care had been expensive and heart-wrenching: I blamed the stress of my absence for the flipped switch on his immune system.

The shock of Kelly's death hung suspended like a body beneath ice. For weeks, I was haunted by images of her end: how Nassir had carried her body around in the chaotic aftermath of the disaster, trying to find help and get word to her family. How she'd been discovered—clutching the hand of a small child.

I spent a dark New Year's, defiantly saying good riddance to my fortieth year with my middle finger raised, feeding Elvis bits of grilled rosemary lamb from my fingertips as I gulped a blood-red Syrah. I wrote down all the things I vowed to leave behind—loss, despair, a creeping belief in futility, working so damn hard—and cast them into the woodstove. I would have a new beginning, *goddamnit*. I would leave it all behind.

But as I entered the darkest part of the year, winter burrowed into my skin—in the roughness of my hands, on my lips and nose, so chapped I'd wake at night because breathing was painful. I was thirsty all the time. I couldn't seem to drink enough water. The air in the cabin crackled along with the constant fire; everything I touched produced a shock. A roasting pan full of water I'd placed on the woodstove was bone dry in an hour. I let the hot shower run with the bathroom door wide open and vented the dryer inside the cabin to put back some of the moisture sucked out by the stove's heat.

The cabin groaned with wind. It slammed into the walls like a tidal wave, sometimes blowing the front door wide open in the middle of the night, hoisting me from sleep and depositing me on a miserably sleepless shore. Those nights were jagged. Outside, lodgepole twirled on their axes as branches snapped loose, while inside, I slept with a pillow over my head to drown out the rushing, train-like sound. More than once, I woke to the fine needle of snow on my face, blown through the cracks in the wall above my bed on arctic air. In the morning, my breath hung cloud-like in the cabin because I could not bring myself to sleep with a fire burning in the house. I was living on the edge of the world.

I'd begun waking up to my heart jump-started by the jolt of some forgotten dream, only to lie suspended between terror and panic, as the thumping in my chest pounded out the dark early-morning hours. Sometimes the beat tapped in quick 2/2 time, as I tried to slow my breathing; other times, it was an earthen boom that shook my chest. As imaginary ghosts paraded across the disasterscape in my mind, I worried that something was wrong with my heart.

Then, I was served papers in a lawsuit over the burned cabin the same week in late January when my mother suffered a massive stroke caused by a giant brain aneurysm. I was flattened.

In her bed in ICU, my mother had the look of a woman straddling two worlds. Everything about her was tentative. The body I knew with its thin ankles and wrists, its hipless waist was present, but another deeper part resisted. A part that wanted nothing to do with oxygen pumps and tubes delivering morphine and blood thinners, a part that had really never wanted anything to do with this life. It was the specter from my childhood.

I knew the instant I saw her she didn't want to live. She hadn't really for years. Life had been a huge disappointment, something to be endured rather than embraced. Mom had struggled too often to simply survive and it had worn her thin. I held her hand, trying to give her some of my strength and determination. Despite everything, I still had will to spare.

"It will be okay," I said, but her pale blue eyes were distant. The aneurysm was a walnut pulsing at the center of her brain. It battered her ocular nerve and forced one eye downward. Mom tried to say something and then closed her eyes, lips tightly pressed. "What?" I asked. Weakly, she shook her head from side to side.

I'd driven two hundred miles that day with my sister, Nancy. Gray snow spit from above as we rushed to Colorado Springs, where my mother lived, only to find she had been airlifted to a neurology unit in Denver. It took hours to locate her. And then, we were told the aneurysm might still burst, she could have another stroke. If my mother survived, the aneurysm would have to be fixed and she would need extensive rehabilitation for her balance and mobility, and help with her follow-up care. That meant she would need to move closer to Nancy, Chris, and me, all living in Boulder County. She was only sixty-three.

My younger brother, Steve, flew in from Salt Lake and joined the rest of us at the hospital, where quite suddenly we were tossed back into the crucible of family. My siblings and I were not close. We'd tried to make alliances over the years, to erase the toxic shadow of our childhood, but being around each other brought out the worst. This was especially true for Chris and me, part of an ongoing grudge match. I was furious it had taken him a month to call me to see if I was okay after my house burned down, and he had long kept a laundry list of transgressions involving my bullish nature. Still, I could not account for the rage he had toward me. He said I was bossy and combative. Sure I was—a hex against the spell cast for me as a girl, my reaction to the assumption that I should follow instead of lead. When the four of us convened in the ICU waiting room, my brothers put their heads together like two CEOs and formulated a plan, leaving my sister and me standing outside the boardroom. While Nancy timidly skirted the periphery, I charged right in.

"What about . . . ?" I demanded repeatedly. In a flash, how to proceed escalated into all-out war. Honestly, it would have been easier to get four strangers to decide how best to help my mother.

For nearly a month in the dark late winter, I drove the three-hour round-trip to Denver three or four times a week, Elvis in tow, to sit with my mother. By the time she was discharged to a rehabilitation facility in Boulder, where she would learn to stand and walk again, it was clear Mom, who could no longer work or drive a car, would have to go on disability. Chris reluctantly split the major responsibilities with me: I took over my mother's medical care while he handled the finances.

Everything during those months was a struggle: I fought with Chris, with social security, with doctors over care and length of stays, and with the insurance company over the burned house.

To people I cooked for at the Merc, I was the girl getting sued.

Some shook their heads and looked askance, others kept their mouths uncharacteristically shut.

"Yeah, I heard about that," said JoJo, who had an opinion on just about everything else, before he changed the subject. It wasn't polite to talk about such things, though I knew the town well enough to know that whispers were ricocheting back and forth across the small valley over Jim Creek.

Absurdly, the insurance company claimed I was at fault for leaving a fire burning in a secure woodstove in a cabin heated solely by that same stove on a cold day when the pipes might freeze. On top of what was an already full plate, I added looking for a lawyer. The least expensive attorney was ten times more than I could afford, and no one wanted to take my case on pro bono.

"My advice?" one lawyer said. "Pay them." It didn't matter who was right, he said, what mattered was who had money. "You're getting screwed, no doubt," he said, but the insurance company "was just doing its job." They routinely filed subrogation suits to try to recoup their payouts.

But I had done nothing *wrong*, I explained.

"Doesn't matter," he said.

I hung up and threw the phone into the couch—hard. Elvis looked up from the floor. *I was right, goddamnit.* The suit couldn't possibly stand, because, well: *I. Was. Right.* I pressed on, calling a dozen lawyers, before finding one who said no and then called me back. She wanted to help but couldn't afford to take me on for nothing. I told her I could scrape together about a thousand dollars.

We struck a deal: I would work on my own case, doing research and assisting her, to offset expenses.

Her advice was to countersue: "Put pressure on the insurance company." Maybe they would drop everything or maybe I could recoup some of my losses, she said, and then mentioned an amount that would level my immediate debt.

For a little while I was full of Erin Brockovich chutzpah—*No one would bully me*. I burned with hope. I could practically hear the soundtrack swelling toward a redemptive end, even though when it was all said and done my naïveté would thunk me right between the eyes. I hadn't the first idea of how the law worked, and unlucky for me, neither did the lawyer who'd come to my aid.

But all of that was in the future; it would take a year before the suit resolved. In the meantime, in the worst part of winter, I woke more and more often to my rattling heart, now amplified by the onset of shivering. My body felt electric, jangling as I pulled the comforter up to my ears and tucked it around my feet, curling myself into a ball. But I couldn't stop the ripples shooting up and down my limbs. *Breathe*, I told myself. I began to whimper. Elvis popped his head up and then came to the side of the bed to see what the matter was. I opened the covers and he climbed in. Unusual, even if it only lasted for ten minutes before he climbed back down: Too hot.

Against the surge of panic, I shoved my pillow near the foot of the bed and crawled through the blankets toward Elvis, throwing my arm out over the edge of the mattress to hook my hand around his chest. Pulling the comforter back around me, I matched my breath to his own. He'd become *my anchor,* the cord that kept me tethered to the earth.

I made a habit of sleeping at the opposite end of the bed, so I could rest my hand on Elvis' slumbering body. It would only occur to me much later that my body was saturated with grief. I'd taken everything in, believing the myth of my invincibility, and bulldozed a path through all that had happened. I never imagined that eventually, I'd have to *feel* anything. Instead I had it all down in the story I told myself and others, in the way I nimbly labeled and analyzed the series of events as if they had happened to someone else.

I drank more frequently and became the kind of person who gets emotional after a few glasses of wine. My sister first noticed it. "Careful, you're turning into Dad," she giggled over lunch. Our father had a reputation for surging displays when he drank, which was fairly often.

"You know you don't have to do anything," said a therapist— one of several I'd seen that year—after I'd delivered yet another half-comical monologue infused with mock outrage at the plot twists in my life.

"Just sit," she said.

For once, I took someone's advice.

In February, each morning, before coffee, before the fire, I sat in bed and silently repeated the mantra that had been given to me over a decade before. Elvis curled up at the edge of my folded legs, protectively.

I have never been a dreamy spaced-out meditator. Sitting has always been like being on a roller coaster—my mind yanks and drops, lunges and banks, while I try to follow the mantra instead. Most mornings, it was like the lid on a garbage can coming off: Out poured all kinds of rotten stuff.

But it *was* a relief. I began to feel a sliver of calm at the edge of my days. I read Stevens' poem out loud after I meditated. I wanted so badly to have *a mind of winter*. Perhaps for just a moment, on those mornings, I did.

Over time, through repetition and seasons, and what was at first a kind of forced surrender, I would learn what it means to be human at the hands of winter. It came to me after I stopped fighting, after I simply stopped, and crawled inside the skin of silence. Then, the bare trees against the sky became a wordless koan, a paradox and a meditation.

In that distant future, one morning, out before dawn in the shivery early light of a late-winter sky to get my paper, I watched a satellite break up, shedding parts like incandescent jewels, across the star-filled horizon. Snow lay sparkling beneath a full moon and the whole of sky and land shimmered silver and white. I felt like I'd stepped inside a movie about a frozen magical kingdom—the scene was so fantastic, it couldn't be real. Its price would be the winters I collected, nine months of practicing quiet, practicing stillness, on the top of Overland Mountain.

A few weeks later, as March dawned, I had burned through my oak. Nothing remained but a pile of chips too small to do anything but cause an angry riot in my drafty stove. The pieces ignited fast and too hot, sending flames shooting up the stovepipe, which reddened alarmingly. So I rationed the remainder of my pine—not even a quarter of a cord, enough for a few really cold days in winter when burned alone.

Bundled most days in a sweater and fleece woolie, hat, and sheepskin boots inside the cabin, I waited for thaw.

Chapter 6

Spring

O ne mid-March morning near the end of my second winter on the mountain, I woke to a loud thumping at the wood box on the deck beneath the front window. Over the winter, I'd gotten in the lazy habit of leaving a trash bag stowed in it overnight before I trudged through the snow to the shed where it was stored until the next trip to town. Usually, the trash froze. And with the exception of a couple of determined ravens and one naughty neighborhood dog who sometimes scattered Brussels sprouts and frozen meat scraps across my deck and into the snow-filled yard like the remnants of a slaughter, I hadn't had a problem.

Elvis looked up half-interested from the indolent pleasure of dog sleep as I bolted from the warmth of my winter-weight down comforter and charged—naked—into the front room, prepared to scold a resolute raven. But when I lifted the prayer shawl over the window, it wasn't the four-pound body of a bird but the three-hundred-pound bulk of a bear. We were nose to nose, separated by eight inches of air on either side of the glass. She looked as startled as me, her back nearly as high as the windowsill. I was always surprised at the size of large mammals—this bear, the buffalo in the Badlands—up close. I banged on the window with the flat of my palm and yelled, "Hey!" The bruin, whose body seemed black and mysterious in the dim light of morning, leaned back then turned, ambling down the steps toward the snow-filled path west, past my truck to the L-shaped curve of the gravel driveway. I grabbed my fleece woolie, a boxy maroon pullover that barely covered my butt, and threw it on, yanking open the door. The bear padded out into the drive as I stepped out of the house and onto the deck on tiptoes to watch her over the rock outcropping ambling along the elbow of the drive south to the road. Then I followed, barefoot, in the thirty-something-degree air and stared as the bear's hind end disappeared in the trees across the dirt road near Paul and Teresa's. The sky was pink and clear and new snow lay on Longs Peak.

Even though the equinox was still more than a week away—and more snow would surely come—it was officially spring.

Spring meant there would soon be pasque flowers circling the peeper pond to the east, even if they had to stubbornly poke their pale violet heads through snow. I would walk the path with Elvis each day, collecting firsts: first tender green in a field of brown; first pasque, first purple vetch; first rosy pack of finches. First morning without a fire in the woodstove. There was so much pleasure in the season. I wanted to take it all in.

Like the bear, I was ready to emerge.

It had been a hard couple of years since the fire. First had been my mother's recovery from her stroke the previous year, an aching process in which she learned to stand and walk and feed herself all over again in rehab. When she was strong enough to travel, Chris and I had accompanied her to Arizona to see an aneurysm specialist. Traditionally, her condition would have been treated by surgical placement of a clip meant to seal off the aneurysm, but that procedure would require the removal of my mother's jaw to allow access to the twenty-five-millimeter pocket at the center of her brain. Instead, the specialist would place coils inside the aneurysm through a catheter inserted into my mother's groin. No doubt, the trip was a reckoning, a Hail Mary pass: Coiling was still a relatively new protocol and the aneurysm was one of the largest the doctor had ever seen. Plus, my mother's insurance would not cover the out-of-network specialist—the top guy in the nation; she would go bankrupt when the bills came in—*if she lived*.

Tucson had been excruciating, not for its scorching spring heat or what had by now become a truculent family dynamic among my siblings, but because neither my mother nor my brother wanted me to come. In our family's pecking order, the oldest son was top dog, and my mother looked to Chris to "take care of things." It was not just Chris' job but his prerogative to be in charge. Trouble was, he could be strangely secretive and tight-lipped, mistrusting, even paranoid, of others. Going along with his plan was like sailing dark water on a moonless night. He rowed silently toward the horizon, wearing responsibility like a loaded cannon strapped to his back.

Hopped up on the idea that I could help, and probably desperate, as I always was, to prove my competence, I inserted myself in the plan and insisted that I go too.

"If there's a chance Mom might die," I told Chris, "I am going to be there." Her medical care was *my responsibility*, I insisted.

I was driven not only by duty and sympathy but by honest concern that my minimalizing mother would deflect and defer and my buttoned-down brother wouldn't see the signs. Plus, he was no caregiver. My mother had spent the six weeks since she'd been discharged from the rehab facility camped out in a hospital bed in his living room while, ridiculously, Nancy and I had to take turns driving from our respective homes in other towns to do Mom's laundry and deliver groceries. Chris worked sixty hours a week to support his wife and two teenage boys—no doubt his plate was full. But about that time, my relationship with my brother went from poor to putrid, fueled by wild stories painting me as a brazen opportunist hell-bent on seizing every advantage for myself. *I wanted to get my hands on Mom's money* (she had none). There were other accusations. None made sense. The more I tried to convince Chris that I'd not done the things suspected of me, the more suspicious he became.

As an adult, I'd learned to walk away from this kind of crazy— the color of which painted most of my childhood. I remember distinctly the day I realized not all families were like mine, that what passed for normal for us was a cocked and loaded gun. At first I'd felt a gushing relief—*it wasn't me, after all*—but this recognition had been followed by a grief so dark and hollow and black, I thought it would swallow me whole. *This* was my family.

At the clinic, the doctor, a man, spoke directly to Chris, ignoring me, while I took notes. We couldn't even wait in the same room during the surgery. Instead, I sat outside the surgery waiting area in an uncomfortable plastic chair in an empty hallway and tried not to imagine having to deliver the news of Mom's demise to Chris, or the awkwardness of either refusing or being refused comfort. Eight hours later, my mother emerged from surgery, talking about flying over her body and seeing her long-deceased parents standing on the edge of the room.

To our surprise, she was discharged the next day. While Chris tried unsuccessfully to rebook our flight home, my mother and I waited in a strangely humid motel room near the hospital. Chris delivered food before retreating, while I helped my too weak to walk and surgically incontinent mother to the bathroom and changed soiled sheets.

"It's a good thing you're here," she said to me without a hint of irony.

When we returned to Colorado, Mom moved straight in with Nancy, whose boyfriend had moved out. A relief for everyone. Slowly, over the next year, much of her strength returned. She graduated from a walker to a cane, and played computer games to help her memory and problem solving, the areas of her brain affected by the stroke. The situation was a good fit not only for my mother, who needed help with some household chores and getting to the store, but also for Nancy, who couldn't afford the apartment on her own.

The stroke and brain surgery changed my mother. Forced to quit her forty-year smoking habit, Susan emerged: her tamped-down emotional reactions burst forth like bubbles exploding to the surface. She smiled more. And giggled, something I'd never heard. Sappy television and, later, the inauguration of the first African American president made her cry. It was as if my mother had been released into the life she was meant to have. All those years of Finnish stoicism fell like chips from a stone block, revealing the woman inside. She was no longer the same woman who in Arizona had accused me in a puritanical tone of "wanting to go out and drink in a strange town" when I announced, after spending two full days as my mother's nurse in a fifteen-by-twenty-foot motel room, I was going out in search of a much-needed glass of wine.

After Mom's surgery, I'd spent the rest of the year—summer to mid-February—working on the lawsuit over the Bar-K cabin. Hopped up on my counsel's bad advice, I'd pressed forward even when the insurance company dropped their suit—the goal all along—a week before trial. I should have cut my losses then. But I'd come too far, I reasoned, and so brimming with the full weight of the injustice of what had happened, I ended up in a courtroom telling the story of the fire in front of a jury, which included three Boulder landlords, on—of all days—the second anniversary of the incident. Prevented from knowing that I had been sued and sued first, the jury saw me as abdicating my responsibility in the matter: I had not had renter's insurance. When I'd started renting at nineteen, no one did. In the end, I was awarded twelve hundred dollars in a split decision because I *should have known better than to start a fire and leave*. Hindsight says I had absolutely no business trying to go hand to hand with a big insurance company. But I had always been a fighter—it was what had gotten me through.

*   *   *

Surely the bear was a sign. The ink on my settlement had been dry for just ten days. I went inside and took down the pumice fetish I'd pulled from the wreckage of the fire. It was a tall, thin bear, black and bladelike, standing upright. A crack from the fire radiated from the center of its chest outward. As I turned the bear over in my hand, it fell into two pieces, dividing the head from the body just where the heart would be.

When I first moved to Jamestown and the Ward Street house with Elvis, I began marking the bear's return each spring by flipping a two-faced hoop hung in my bedroom. On the winter side, the leather was white with a small alabaster bear fetish tied to the center. In spring, the face was painted black, with small gold bear tracks. Following bears had been my way of keeping track of seasons and sensibility: Winters, the ritual reminded me, were quiet and contemplative—I'd hole up with books and movies and take long naps—while summers were playful and singing, for making tracks, as Elvis and I hiked and camped, and I watched things grow. I hadn't practiced the ritual since the hoop burned in the fire two years before. I simply hadn't had the heart. For too long, I realized,

I had been reluctant to do anything—write, celebrate the season—
that would tie me to the excruciating present.

I wondered suddenly if the morning's bear was the same I'd
encountered the summer I moved into the cabin. If so, we had
weathered the same seasons. We shared landscape, the same night
skies. I wondered where it slept in the winter, where it found food
now in the spring. Did the bear take seasons of drought or wildfire
or lack of food personally? I was certain the answer was no.

It was time to stop holding my breath, time to put the fire and
its aftermath—loss, my mother's illness, the lawsuit—behind me.
Carefully, I glued the bear back together and then lit a little sage,
and brushed the smoke in swirls around the rough pumice in my
palm. An ancient ritual. Even the Catholic Church used incense
for purification and blessing. In some masses it was said to be the
prayers of the faithful rising to heaven.

Sometimes I needed to be reminded that I have always believed
in rebirth.

Determined to get on with it, I stood the pumice bear on the altar
beneath the bookshelf, letting the sage burn on a stone next to it,
and said a little prayer for bear and for our shared season to come.

Whether you can bring yourself to hope for it or not, things
change. The seasons remind us of that. The deep snow of winter
only seems like it lasts forever, but soon enough the first robin
appears like a russet blotch on a white field, followed by the miracle
of bluebirds the color of the astonishing Colorado sky. Bears wake
up hungry and stalk the meadows for last year's berries and any

patch of green. They'll eat larvae and bugs and even live chickens, as one of my neighbors discovered when the unsecured pen she'd erected in her yard in the winter was rolled across the road and into the meadow, leaving chicken carcasses in its wake. Soon enough, ground squirrels would reappear, crawling up from their winter dens. I watched one lazy dreamer I called Romeo stretch languorously and look out wistfully over the edge of my wooded lot each day in an afternoon patch of sun on the rock outside my kitchen window. In the mornings, I woke to a single robin calling the sun awake with its urgent, happy song. Soon more summer birds—hummers and pine siskin, swallows, grosbeak, and tanager—would return. Another season would begin—this one brief—pitted with wild storms that could dump as much as four feet of wet snow—and for this very reason, perhaps all the more precious. I would take the shifting landscape as a sign. Change would come.

*   *   *

In a gesture of wild hope, I hung out my hummingbird feeders the first week of April even though it would probably be a couple of weeks before I heard the telltale trill on the mountain. The sound, which always gave my heart a small jolt, was one of the happiest tunes I knew—like joy announcing its return across a browned-out meadow.

On the day in mid-April when I saw a tiny green female sipping tentatively from the red-mouthed feeder, I got in the truck and drove straight down to Boulder to buy pansies, flowers that would last all spring and summer at altitude. I liked hot colors—subterranean violets mixed with apricot—but in a delirium of spring fever, I couldn't resist buying some freakish-looking black and blood-red varieties, pairing them with an angelic white tinged at the heart with pale yellow.

At home, I unloaded the flat of pansies and unearthed my pots—three clay window boxes, two shallow footed bowls, and a strawberry pot—from the shed, which, to my surprise, a squirrel had annexed over the winter. There were cached pinecones in every open box, between boards and walls, inside my frame pack, and even in the repair bag on my bike—hundreds, enough to fill a fifty-gallon trash can by the time I'd collected them all and plugged the hole between the roof and rafters. An hour later, I'd filled the clay pots with pansies and the railing along my deck was a riot of color in the dun-shaded landscape.

At night, I would have to lug all six containers inside as the temperatures hovered near thirty, but the work was worth it as light cascaded over my abridged rainbow in the afternoon while a squirrel hopped from the cairn of pinecones I'd left behind the shed across a patch of snow.

Warmer daytime temperatures revealed the hopeful white blossoms of mouse-ear and heralded the return of the spring peepers, infinitesimally small frogs who lived in the pond just a quarter mile from the cabin. I heard them in the dusk of late April, a gentle sleigh-bell-like song that followed me as I fell asleep. The evenings would be full of their singing until the end of May, when mating was done. The pond expanded, soaking the edges of the walking path with snowmelt, making puddles in small pockets around a few pine trees. A mating pair of mallards glided in the water, a basin as big as the clearing that shrunk as the water of spring thaw receded and reeds and minty-smelling lake grass filled the wetlands. I knew then it was time to begin contemplating the garden.

The previous summer, I had cleared an S-shaped bed between the barely-there stone walkway leading to my deck to the south and the northern edge of the five-foot-high rock outcropping, lining it with hand-sized clay tiles arranged diamond-like so their points touched. In the belly of the S, I made a circle from broken persimmon- and rose-colored Fiesta ware salvaged from the Bar-K cabin. Into this fiery pink and orange sun, I had hopefully planted a lavender that hadn't survived the winter. While my preference was to fill my garden with sun-loving plants like echinacea, California poppy, and coreopsis, my impossible high-altitude plot, centered beneath three aspen trees, caught mostly shade.

When I lamented to my new Jamestown friend Judith, a woman with spiky gray hair and eyes that crinkled happily when she grinned, that shade plants were boring, she rolled her eyes. Her own garden was a Jamestown legend.

"It's about texture, not color, darling. We can fix *that*," she said. A Brit who'd grown up memorizing and reciting poems in postwar England, Judith spoke the words roundly, as if she was tasting each as it exited her mouth. My own speech, by comparison, was a slur and a growl.

We'd met the previous summer when she sauntered into the Merc in orange harem pants and a lime-green tank top and pink scarf to buy a single cigarette—"My one vice," she announced—and we had one of the funniest conversations I've ever had involving hedgehogs, dirty laundry, scones (pronounced *scons*), the pleasures of swearing (for me) and rhyming poetry (for her). By the end, she'd invited me to tea.

A week later, I sat in her garden, a spectacular patch that cascaded from the lip of Mesa Street in Jamestown, halfway down an embankment toward Jim Creek, populated with painted stones, small curiosities, and things her children had made. Two large arcing walls fashioned by her sculptor and builder husband, David, divided the garden into tiers. A stone path led to the house in one direction and David's workshop and a small lawn in the other, where she hung laundry in the summer. Judith was a tender of beauty: She showed me a climbing rose called Don Juan—"a bit of a prima donna"—that produced sometimes only a single rose in a season. Her garden contained such rarities along with medicinal herbs like feverfew and echinacea for tinctures. Vegetables grew in a hoop house on the best patch of sun.

She'd met David when he lived in a tent on the land in the seventies and moved in with him almost immediately while he built the workshop, the first structure on the property. The house came next: There was a tower and spiral stair and a living room Judith called the "cave" because three sides were sunk into the canyon wall for insulation and the roof grew violets. The upstairs bath had a floor-to-ceiling window that overlooked the garden, the other three walls painted a luminous edge-of-spring green. Tiny stars glowed on the ceiling. Art hung on the walls—pieces made by Judith and her children and artists from the area. Judith made the kind of home I would if I was half as organized and ten times less messy. If I ever settled somewhere long enough.

Judith turned out to be my twin in temperament—brash, bawdy, outspoken, wild. I loved her instantly. That spring, she announced that she would relieve me of my shade plant prejudice by bringing me plants from her own ample garden on my birthday.

Elvis ran excitedly back and forth, charging ahead of us from Judith's car to the yard as we carried containers full of fuzzy lady's mantle and monkshood, two types of lavender because Judith said "It's worth a try," a couple of white campanulas, an emerald-leafed Turkish veronica, a hellebore that would bloom a greenish pink the following March, and an ornamental oregano, which Judith proclaimed would grow anywhere—"even in this puny plot." I added a Cupid's dart and some violets I'd picked up.

The mid-May morning was blue and clear and above us, the aspens were just opening into the kind of green that glows. Judith, dressed in vine and brown harem pants with a black tank beneath a white shirt, sang sea shanties and dug in compost while I dug out the amber roots of aspen snaking through the plot. I've always loved getting dirty. It felt good to put my hands in the earth even though the blackened crescents beneath my fingernails would require some scrubbing. The air smelled of freshly thawed soil, still damp and rich. Pine siskins cheeted in the fir where the feeder was hung. Elvis settled at the steps, watching from above.

When we finished planting, Judith ceremoniously marched back to her car and returned singing, "Happy birthday to you, Happy birthday, dear Ka-ren!" In her hands, she carried a small gold plate that held patches of moss and pebbles, a few strange coins, and tiny pieces of mica. In the center sat the two-inch-high figure of Amaterasu, the Japanese sun goddess, the bestower of grace. A sliver of wood served as her staff. It was one of Judith's goddess gardens—I had admired several she had placed in and out of her house, the biggest of which sat next to her door, made from palm-size pieces of moss dug from her own garden and stones her children had given her. On it, a five-inch-tall Vesta, the Roman goddess of home and hearth.

"She reminds me of Mary," said Judith, looking at Amaterasu.

"The virgin or the whore?" I asked, making a face.

Judith shook her head. "No, the Mary of the pietà. The Mary of compassion."

"It's the most beautiful thing anyone has ever made me," I said.

I put the goddess garden on the glass table on the deck, where it would live out of doors all summer before being moved to my writing desk in winter.

I filled two champagne flutes with bubbly and Chambord, and Judith and I raised our glasses to the new garden and my forty-second year as we ate shrimp cakes I'd made, along with a salad of mixed greens topped with green apples and pecans. Judith read a favorite poem, Naomi Shihab Nye's "Kindness"—"Before you know what kindness really is / you must lose things"—and we exchanged bear stories.

"Just yank your skirt up when you see one," she said. "They won't attack a woman."

"Right." I laughed. "Because both of us so often trot through the meadow in a dress—Where the hell did you get that one?"

Judith shrugged. "Women and bears," she said, "that's an old story, dearie."

I thought of a story Judith had told me about gardening by candlelight, wearing a pelt-like blanket over her shoulders. "I almost want to grunt doing it," she said gleefully.

Later in the afternoon, after Judith waved goodbye, it began to rain, a cold spring rain that slapped the newly turned dirt in the garden. I closed the cabin windows and watched the air go slushy. A curtain of ice and rain descended, collecting in clumps along the path. By dark, fat-wet flakes fell and I ran outside to cover the new plants with a tarp, tenting the Cupid's dart. When I woke the next morning, three inches of fresh snow blanketed the garden and the Cupid's dart's long stalk had broken.

"I guess we were a little eager," said Judith.

* * *

In early June, a bear got into the grease bucket outside the Merc, an oil drum that stored old fryer lard and the blackened contents of the flattop's drawer-like trap. The bear overturned the drum, spilling grease out into the main street of Jamestown. You could see its oily paw prints drifting up the road before turning toward Anderson Hill and the northern edge of town. Jamestown's message board, the QT, lit up with posts about sightings and keeping the bears safe by keeping trash out of their way. Trouble was, not everyone paid attention, and at least one house on the edge of town was rumored to feed the bears outright. I worried about the bear who probably figured it had found a good deal—so many hummingbird feeders and trash cans or cars with dog food and leftover fast-food sacks in one relatively small spot. Stories where bears routinely encounter humans always end badly for the bear. And as if the future was one of those books whose ending we'd all already read, after repeated break-ins to cars and people's homes, the bear was put down by the Division of Wildlife because it was deemed a "nuisance."

I left my shift at the Merc that night after watching the green DOW vehicle loaded with the bear's body drive out of town and raised a sad glass of wine to the stars as I watched the Big Dipper slide toward the horizon.

Over the seasons I spent at the cabin, I would talk to bears passing through, toast them with wine from the deck, see them scramble up hillsides when I hiked, and find evidence of their day beds in the narrow ravine near the spring. I've heard them passing through in the dark on warm summer nights when I slept with my head inches from the open window and was comforted to live in a place where such things were possible.

*   *   *

That spring, I placed my own foot firmly in the Jamestown community. I'd been circling the town periphery for a few years, flipping pancakes at the benefit breakfast on the Fourth of July and entering and losing the annual pie contest every single year, even hosting a few poetry nights at the Merc for Poets Against the War, but my participation was always measured, tentative. I showed up. And then I retreated.

For a year, I'd been thinking about joining the town's art organization—JAM (Jamestown Area Artists and Musicians). Trouble was the emphasis seemed to be on the musicians. Most of the events in town were related to music—Java JAM (an acoustic coffeehouse in the park) and Band in a Hat (an event that put impromptu bands together from a drawing). JAM's regular meetings often erupted in jam sessions, turning them into parties with bong hits and bottles of beer. I know I wasn't the only one who was put off by the let's-drink-some-beer-and-play! mentality; if you didn't sing, pick, or pound, you *watched*.

Clearly, JAM had a PR problem.

In its decade-long history, the organization had single-handedly supported improvements to the historic town hall—purchase of quilted window coverings, a stage, lights, and microphones— things that made the dim, drafty stone building dating back to 1935 functional as both a gathering place for town meetings and for entertainment, so they did good things. *But what about the*

"Artists" in Jamestown Area Artists and Musicians? I thought. There were plenty of them living in the area—a Buddhist stone carver, several painters, an installation artist who had work in an L.A. gallery, writers, jewelry makers, a potter, and even a filmmaker. JAM could do better.

Finally after talking to Chad, one of the cooks at the Merc who had been on the JAM board, I screwed up my courage and attended a meeting at Nancy Farmer's robin's-egg-blue house across the street from Joey and his lawn full of pink flamingos, armed with ideas about how JAM could represent everyone in town. I'd long known Nancy as the matriarch of a family of singers, her bell-like voice clear as mountain air. Like the rest of the town, I'd watched her daughters grow from giggling girls to young women who sang just as sweetly as their mother.

At the meeting, I knew everyone by name and a few by reputation: I'd seen Hortense, JAM's president, in a couple of scene-chewing performances at the town hall. Although she registered tilt on the enthusiasm meter, she could neither act nor carry a tune. But that was the fun of small-town stuff, I suppose. Everyone got to play.

Once Hortense announced "new business," Chad pointed to me. I tried to gingerly raise the idea of getting more artists involved. My idea, I said, was to increase JAM's visibility by sponsoring other events.

First was Poetry Night at the Merc.

"All you have to do is let me put your logo on the flyer," I said, "and lend me a mic and amp. People will see you doing more in town." Michael, an original board member, and bearded drummer of a much beloved local band called The Neighbors, offered his equipment. The proposal passed easily.

Next: *What about sponsoring a series of what I called Master Classes given by artists in town?* Anyone could attend for ten dollars and the proceeds would be split between JAM and the artist. I'd already lined up a local painter and a dancer. I would arrange everything, I assured them, but I needed JAM's sponsorship to use the town hall without the required rental fee. Maybe I was a bit ballsy. But it wasn't in my nature to simper and suggest. I saw ways to help, and once I'd decided to do so, I leapt into the fray.

The discussion about the classes stretched out for an hour. Members squabbled over the name ("*master* is off-putting"), how much money to give to artists ("They should volunteer, *we do*"), and how many classes to hold ("You don't want to bore people").

Clearly, I'd stomped on some toes.

But suddenly I didn't care. Perhaps opposition was the thing I needed to push against to allow me to stop standing on the edge. I'd planted myself on Overland Mountain and now I was claiming more ground.

In that meeting, I decided: It was my town too.

*   *   *

I never worried about bears breaking into the house, even though the possibility certainly existed. Whether this fact made me fearless or stupid, I don't know. Of course I had Elvis, who growled at who-knew-what was prowling around outside at night; by the time I'd open the door, it was long gone. Only once did a bear try to get into the shed where I stored the trash. It ripped a foot-long piece of siding from the door and pulled the padlock away but couldn't make the door open.

When I was young, I cut my teeth on tales of Yogi and Smokey and my favorite, Baloo, whose strength and size impressed me as much as his southern drawl. I loved my father's early-morning accounts of the cinnamon brown cub that circled our camp, leaving jaw marks in an empty Styrofoam bottle packer left out on the picnic table. As an adult, I loved the bear's mystery: It spends half its year denned up, inhabiting the liminal space between seasons, and maybe, as mystics and poets tell us, dreaming in the half-waking light of winter.

"The bear is a dark continent / that walks upright / like a man," writes Chickasaw poet Linda Hogan, pointing not only to the bear's physical presence but also to the kinship between bears and humans. It's well known that bear skeletons resemble our own; according to Hogan, it is only *human* fear and, most of all, cruelty that separate us.

When I saw my first grizzly bear in Yellowstone, I cried. I was in my late twenties. My friend Julie and I had come down a mountain pass on the east side of the park, after a thunderstorm. We knew a buffalo herd grazed the grasslands below. The sky to the south was black with weather, and we were pressing into it, but overhead the clouds pulled apart like cotton balls and pockets of light splashed down on the valley. I'd swung my head to the side, tracking a big bird, when I saw them—a pair of two-year-olds, we'd been told, turning rocks not far from the road, their shoulders and front paws dipped in honey. It was September. My family was gathering back in Colorado for a reunion to celebrate Grandpa Pete's eightieth birthday, an event to which I had not been invited, owing to my estrangement from my father and my grandfather's ongoing fury that I'd changed my last name.

Julie pulled her pickup truck over to the side of the road, and I dug out the binoculars. I couldn't believe the size of the bears' claws or the rocks they upended, the ease with which they exhibited such strength. My own shows of force were exactly that—messy, disruptive, pushy.

Julie and I watched the bears for a long time as the wind swirled among the tall grass and the sun sank. There was something elemental about coming into the presence of a big predator. It was more than awe. I had the feeling of being picked up and deposited back in my place among the stars; I was no more and no less than the rest of it. But, make no mistake, I was a part of it.

Maybe that's why mountain living suited me. My life at the cabin was ordered by weather and wildlife. I could let the thousand distractions of the modern world fall away. I couldn't pretend that what was happening outside my window didn't affect me.

In this way, the great catastrophe of the fire was also its greatest gift: It had pared everything away. No doubt, it had been a rocky few years as I scrambled over ledges without the relative comfort or distraction of material goods, alone on the mountain. But being stripped of everything let me make my own path into a place where the natural world and the world I lived in were not separate. I didn't want to view nature as something *out there*. Instead, like a bear denning for winter, I wanted to climb inside.

Chapter 7

Summer

Summer warmed suddenly, as it often did. One day was spring with lilacs and forsythia popping out along the apron of mountains that led to the plains, and the next, the temperature blasted into the eighties. Up on Overland Mountain, after weeks of ululating highs, the days quite suddenly shifted to a perfect seventy-eight degrees, wildflowers exploding in the meadow behind the cabin and around the peeper pond. As people in Boulder sweltered in near-ninety-degree heat almost three thousand feet down-canyon, I stalked the meadows with Elvis in temperate air, collecting flowers for my notebook: the soft fuzzy heads of pussytoes, which looked exactly like delicate cat paws; the lemony, pod-like flowers of golden banner; or the faded purple of lupine. Beneath each variety, flattened and taped to the page, I wrote its name and the date in an honest attempt to get to know my neighbors.

When I'd first moved to the Bar-K cabin, staking my claim on landscape was the equivalent of stubbornly planting a flag and proclaiming territory. It was an act of conquest: I would seize the wild. I'd gotten exactly what I'd asked for: the unharnessed life I'd sought shoved its way into view the day my house burned down. I didn't know then the strength of my own desire.

I've never been someone who takes the easy road. Something in my body gravitates toward rocks and sharp edges, toward storms and umbrage. The summer I spent living in the tent in James Canyon after I'd changed my name, I decided what I needed was a few nights alone on a mountaintop contemplating my soul. I would fast and sleep out in the open. So I set off with a rain tarp and some water, and climbed straight out of the gulch to the top of Castle Peak, pulling myself hand over foot up its steep face, trying not to look down or think of falling. It was August hot, and by the time I reached the summit, I had drunk most of my water. That evening, a thunderstorm rolled in. As I watched lightning flick and stab, moving closer and closer, I realized I was sitting on the highest point in any direction. Unwilling to give up, I lay flat on the ground and sang to the storm.

The next day, out of water, I returned early along a path I'd discovered on the back side of the mountain that meandered sweetly into the gulch.

I'd softened a bit over the years; now I wanted kinship not conquest. At the High Lake cabin, I wanted to become part of the pattern, the passage of seasons. So I wrote it all down: the first pasque to the final purple aster that bookended the growing season; the weasel who lived beneath the house and turned snow white in winter; the chipmunk who led her pups to drink rainwater from a basin carved out of a rock just east of the garden; the two pine siskins I drove to the wildlife rehabilitation center after I found them sluggish beneath the bird feeder. Over time, I'd fill notebooks with what I saw, and in those details grew the story I shared with Overland Mountain.

Don't try to write the poem about love, I often tell my students. *Write the poem about making apple galette for your lover. Or about your grandfather's hands as he ties flies. Let love rise out of the details.* So I collected plants and weather, wildlife and birds, and in between the spaces of my notebook, love rose like a fish to the surface, like clouds of pine dust in air.

*   *   *

The garden Judith and I planted was beginning to take root. Lady's mantle fanned out along the fattest edge of the bed, presenting wide, palm-size leaves, and the oregano flourished, sending up deep blue-green tendrils. Nearby, purple-tinged veronica had begun its long, slow bloom, like a Polaroid coming into focus.

Judith was right: What the garden lacked in flamboyant color, it made up for in charm and magic. The lady's mantle collected droplets of moisture like shimmering translucent stones after a good rain, and the light splashed across plant stems and leaves was ever-changing, filtered through the two large aspens just off the deck. I placed a pine stump that curled onto itself like a heart upright near the rock outcropping that divided the yard from the driveway just at the thinnest part of the garden's S shape, where a trio of smaller aspens met. On top of the stump was a flat palm-size geode whose "window" was clouded over, another fire remnant. A reminder of how I got here. A testament to the unknown and unknowable forces of nature.

Nearby, a steer skull lay among finger sage and white yarrow, natural volunteers that grew along the curve of its horns. I had learned to let nature make its offerings. So kinnikinnick and a bit of lichen-covered stone infiltrated the shallow rock-filled soil near the stump, and marigold-orange wallflowers sprouted along the edges.

On the solstice, Elvis and I encountered a curious coyote, who stepped absentmindedly between two junipers toward us as I sat in the late afternoon of the longest day near an overlook just past the peeper pond. I had discovered a roughened stone spiral in a grouping of rocks and gathered more to fill in its gaps—my own personal semaphore—to welcome summer, whose official arrival, I mused, marked the now dwindling days. The spiral contained the mystery of that contradiction—a beginning that presaged an end, the ever-changing flux of seasons—but it also recalled my hard and soft edges, the unraveling I had begun to feel. Not the unraveling of the fire, the way I'd been shorn of everything but grief, but the unraveling of fists held tight for too long, of borders becoming porous, my body slackened, opening to pleasure. I was staring at the spiral's arms radiating out and radiating in when the coyote came into view.

The animal's mottled gray and russet fur blew in scruffy patches along her neck; long legs dangled loosely from her body. Her eyes were gold. Gently, I put out my hand to hold my dog's harness.

Elvis' ears moved forward and his tail made a friendly swish in the dirt, but he didn't so much as growl. "It's okay," I breathed. Even he sensed the extraordinary nature of what was happening. Fifteen feet away, the coyote took four automatic steps toward us before she saw us. Clearly, she'd come this way before. As fluidly as she'd appeared, she disappeared, turning with neither alarm nor hubbub, angling back over the small rise.

Just another animal in the landscape.

*   *   *

To friends off the mountain, I was in peril. I lived outside a presumed net of safety—one knit together by proximity to society—people, hospitals, law enforcement—things it was implied that as a woman, I required.

"I don't know where you get this," my citified grandmother said when I recounted a bear story or when I lit out for territory with Elvis, as if I'd developed a sudden appetite for eating animal carcasses and wearing pelts. This from the woman whose husband had herded sheep in Utah by himself when he was fourteen. *It was in my blood.*

I would take my chances with nature any day. There was an open-door policy on the mountain, and like a lot of people, I left my door unlocked whether I was home or not. Joey kept the key to the Merc above the front door, a habit that occasionally resulted in folks helping themselves to coffee or cigarettes. Karen Z stored the keys to her pickup in the ignition of her unlocked vehicle. I liked living in a place where it wasn't necessary to bolt the door, where I didn't feel a dangerous *someone* was outside trying to get in.

Naïvely, I'd carried this attitude with me when I left Jamestown the first time for Milwaukee, a city where doors were necessarily secured and chained. The second week I was there, someone swiped my Gore-Tex shell through the open slider window of my locked truck. And in my most embarrassing Rebecca of Sunnybrook Farm moment, I witnessed a robbery without comprehending what was happening. A man exited my neighbor's house carrying a blue plastic storage bin and disappeared into the alley.

He's doing something he shouldn't, I thought absentmindedly, stirring soup on the stove. Twenty minutes passed before it occurred to me to call the police, and then I had to explain, red-faced, to the responding officers why it had taken me so long to report the crime.

I was golden in nature, a rube in the city.

Even if I was living in some remote wilderness—and I wasn't by any stretch of the imagination—I was *safe,* from the ancient root *sol,* meaning whole. And I found my wholeness is solitude and space. "Everything in nature," says the writer Gretel Ehrlich, "invites us constantly to be what we are." Not *who* but *what.* On the most basic level, I was landscape too. Even though my intention in moving to the mountains may have been rooted in escape, the natural world coaxed me back into myself. It wasn't unlike what Hindu mystics tell us happens to the self over time with meditation practice. You learn to let everything drop away. Ehrlich says it this way: "We are often like rivers: careless and forceful, timid and dangerous, lucid and muddied, eddying, gleaming, still." We are all that and none of it at all.

*   *   *

A week after the solstice, Elvis and I hiked east past the peeper pond, down a narrow draw that stopped near a spring. Just before the small mud-lined pool, he took an abrupt right turn, climbing an embankment under a downed lodgepole—another path. We must have passed it dozens of times on our way to Overland Mountain, not ten minutes from where I now stood. Curious, I followed my dog through the narrow opening to a small glade. Hundreds of Colorado blue columbine dotted the sides of the thin trail overgrown with rare ferns and wild carrot. Light splashed through tree limbs framing luminous white-faced blossoms strange as orchids.

I felt as if I had stepped into a cool stone church on a hot afternoon. There was a peculiar quiet to the place. Not the quiet of absence, but the quiet of presence, the quiet of magic. The sound of birds chattering fell away and a hush descended like a large cotton cloth falling from a window. Starched white heads fanned with blue were everywhere. I found a spot near the center and sat down, entranced by the place whose sentience was palpable. A remnant of the wild earth.

A slight early-summer breeze made the aspens clack and

rearranged the lacy heads of hemlock in a kind of sinuous dance. Elvis settled into my lap, sitting upright between my crossed legs. He leaned his back into me, giving me his weight, the same way he'd done when I met him for the first time at the animal shelter.

With Elvis, an animal who'd fused himself to me the way I was told wolves do, I moved more instinctually, alert to the things that drew his attention. It was as if the tether I'd used to train him to stay with me had become an extended invisible cord: He was my sixth sense. At first I was simply more aware of whatever could get him killed—ledges, wildlife, hunters with guns—but that awareness deepened to take in texture and sound and smell, the nuances of terrain. With him, I became more present. And now, as it so often had, the feeling of his body next to me anchored me to the physical world, filling me with a calm I seldom felt. My mind wanted too much to go tumbling down the hill, getting ahead of the day and whatever was just beyond the tip of my nose, but the still-wild husky gathered it back. Elvis had long been my eyes, my ears, but now I realized he was also my guru, my guide: His presence reminded me to play now, sleep now, explore now, *be* now.

The fairy forest, with its "dappled things," its "landscape plotted and pieced," would become a kind of secret garden. A place I felt was all my own. We all need ground for stillness. But I wanted beauty too—to gather it in my fists and drag its skirts across the landscape of my days.

* * *

Beauty, I knew, had its own sharp edges. Wildness was a box of unruly, sharp-toothed weasels, a predator that lets its prey bleed to death. Life at the cabin meant contending with the critters who sometimes tried to share my space. In the summer, I routinely battled chipmunks who squirmed beneath the unevenly hung screen door and caused heated games of chase, as I tried to corral them back out before Elvis—who upended chairs and wastebaskets in pursuit—caught them. Despite rolled-up towels weighted and held in place with quart jars filled with beans and steel-cut oats, one managed to work its way in every few weeks. I bore their insurgencies as part of mountain living—just as I tolerated mice.

Up to a point.

I didn't mind the mice running along the wall beneath the bookcase, even though Elvis went wild, becoming the Great White Hunter, sniffing for the creatures long after they had disappeared. In his younger days, I'd seen him pounce on a mouse from twenty feet out on a dark night in a snow-filled field. I had no idea what he was doing until I saw him toss the body up into the air. At the cabin, he frequently convinced me that something was behind all those books on the lowest shelf or inside a stack of newspapers. I'd dutifully unearth papers and books as Elvis nosed toward the back of the shelf, the bottom of the pile, pawing. Inevitably, I'd end up with a mess and no mouse. But they were there: At night, sometimes I'd hear them rattle dishes in the drainer. And I'd let it go.

The cabin was a leaky boat, so poorly put together that it was impossible to seal all the cracks where mice got in, so I lived and let live until the clamor in the kitchen crescendoed into a party that kept me awake or trails of scat in the dark reaches of my food cupboard gave way to worries about hantavirus. Traps laid, I would kill a dozen mice over a period of a few weeks, dutifully marching the dead carcasses out beyond the watering hole rock, where someone—Fox? Raccoon? Coyote?—scooped them up in the night, until the morning I discovered—inevitably—not a dead mouse but a badly injured one, hanging by its foot from the trap, dangled in the thin space between the countertop and fridge. Horrified at the thought of the terrible and terrifying night the mouse had spent, I gingerly released it into a washcloth and placed it in the oak woodpile, along with seeds and a dab of butter before I went inside to put the rest of the traps away, and the whole cycle would repeat itself in six months, when another killing spree would come abruptly to an end with a mutilated rodent.

I was a selective killer to be sure. It wasn't in my nature to hurt things. I carted out spiders and yellow jackets even though I flat-out smashed mosquitoes. The mice and I did our dance season after season. I tried talking to them, as I had heard the poet Audre Lorde did; I tried warning them. But in the end, some would die.

This exertion of territory grew into a war for supremacy that summer when the ground squirrels began systematically dismantling my new garden. I had been ignoring them as they ran across the deck and between the monkshood near the tall rocks at the back of the garden. *What harm could they do?* But then I noticed someone had gone after the herbs I planted in a new larger strawberry pot placed at the top of the steps, nibbling and spitting out rosemary and eating all the tender cilantro. In what I thought was a smart preemptive strike, I covered the pot with deer net. Then I put a tomato cage on the salad container I'd planted and wrapped it in more netting. A scant week later, I found a ground squirrel, a kind of oversized fat-looking chipmunk, hanging from the mesh, almost strangled. Its chest thumped visibly as I carefully cut it from the black netting, all the while trying to avoid its teeth. Once the squirrel was free, I removed the net and cage, and gave up on my salad garden until I could think of a better plan.

I should have known about the deer netting; my uses of it had only ever yielded poor results. I'd once had to perform the same extrication ritual with, of all things, a baby skunk, who'd gotten into the shed at the Bow Mountain house, my first mountain house. The animal was so tangled in deer net that it was encased in clouds of it and a knot as thick as my wrist was bunched like an umbilical cord at its abdomen. I hoisted the creature, no bigger than the size of two fists, by a stick slipped through the netting and with the other hand carefully ran my fingers over its skin to snip at all the places it had gotten tangled, while the skunk took repeated aim at me with its exhausted scent sacs.

Unfortunately the ground squirrel in the salad pot was just the first salvo of an all-out invasion. I returned home from teaching one day to see that my beautiful black pansies had been mowed down and chewed apart. My mantra: *Mountain living*. But then they went after my garden. In a matter of weeks, the violets had been munched along with all the hopeful California poppies I'd planted in my one patch of sun. Then they neatly clipped the only bloom from a chocolate cosmos, a flower that didn't have much of a chance to begin with in my shady plot. I'd rejoiced when I saw the blossom open and then cursed when I found it lying on the ground.

Over the course of a week, anything that was tender and green or had a bud—went. And that's when I went to war.

I tried an assortment of disgustingly scented sprays. One, guaranteed by my favorite garden store, had rancid egg solids—the scent of which was so bad, I gagged when I used it. Hours after application, the smell wafted in the front window of my tiny cabin and I had to retreat to the bedroom. In the garden, I tried coyote piss, my own piss, and even Liquid Fence, which smelled exactly like fish carcasses mixed with something more sinister—an odor I'd encountered on the Milwaukee River when Elvis rolled in something black and slick along its banks and I had to spray everything—including the cleaning towel and my shoes—with Febreze and wash it at least three times before the odor began to recede. I dutifully pumped the perimeter of the garden with the Liquid Fence in the late afternoon, and not two hours later, in the slanted sun of a still bright summer evening, Elvis charged to the screen, growling: My fence had attracted a huge, slow-moving bear to the yard. Out the door without a thought, I picked up some wood chips at the bottom of the steps and threw them at the chest-high beast yelling "Shoo!" The bear turned reluctantly and moved back into the woods beyond the berm. Only after I had returned to the relative safety of my screened-in cabin did I think about what I had done.

Shoo? I said to Elvis, and then shook my head. *Jesus.*

After I'd tried every smelly thing I could think of to get rid of the ground squirrels, I resorted, reluctantly, to traps. My plan was to live-trap and relocate. But the squirrels ran right by the open cage for weeks. The final straw was the day I watched a squirrel put the kibosh on the last campanula, flattening the white-flowered stalks by walking them down—stem to blossom—as I shouted and chased it from the garden. Furious, I marched over to Paul's to borrow the rat trap he'd offered a few weeks before and set it, loaded, just outside the door. Within an hour, I'd caught a squirrel by its paw. I released it and it limped away while I reset the trap. The next day, the squirrel was caught by its neck. I came home from the Merc to find it weakly flailing in the trap. It gazed at me dully; the suffering was plain. Its back leg flopped ineffectually, bent at an odd angle. There was nothing to be done. I depressed the metal hammer, suffocating the creature, whose mouth opened wider and wider, for the longest two minutes of my life. Sickened, I returned the trap to Paul.

"Get him?" he asked. No, I shook my head.

Resigned, I surrendered the garden to the squirrels.

*   *   *

The real beginning of summer in Jamestown was the annual Fourth of July celebration, an event where the whole town pitched in to raise money for the volunteer fire department. It began with a pancake breakfast in the town hall that spilled out into the little park across the street and a parade down Main Street with *El Patrón*'s Model A's, Joey's kazoo band, and kids throwing candy from atop the fire engine. After that, the day continued with food booths and music in the big park called Elysian Fields, at the east end of town, followed by fireworks.

This summer, in addition to the traditional pie- and cake-baking contests, for which the winner won a ribbon, there would be a wood-chopping event that promised a prize of an entire cord of wood. Although plenty of women chopped wood across the mountain, only two entered the contest. Instead, a pack of guys signed up, eager to take a swing. The contest was scheduled for the late afternoon, by which time a good number of people would be deep into celebrating. For this reason, I cringed when I'd heard the announcement and watched breathlessly as a few contestants wielded axes wearing shorts, and others took long swigs from red cups of beer or a pull from JoJo's moonshine flask before heaving the ax skyward.

Of course, the crowd ate it up, cheering loudly for a few of the drunker guys. I kept my fingers crossed for Karen Q, the third Karen in Jamestown, a compact woman who leathered up and rode motorcycles and lived alone in a cabin "up top" without electricity or running water. She was outnumbered seven to one. But I cheered the loudest for Jojo, twenty years the senior of the next oldest person who entered. At seventy-two, he was gray-bearded and bald and wearing a red, white, and blue shirt that matched the one his wife, Jesse, wore. He hacked through each carefully chosen log with one massive swing of the ax. In four rounds, he went head to head and won against Barefoot Kenny; a big hulk of a man named Sean, who wore shorts and nearly gouged his leg; Rudiger, who smiled and missed, smiled and missed; and finally Rod, the toothy, bearded man who'd set up the contest and strutted around as if he was certain to be the winner.

While I chopped wood reluctantly and never for sport, I'd been trying ever since I moved to Jamestown to win the pie contest, and my efforts—Shaker lemon pie, champagne peach with ginger crust—placed but never flat-out won. In what was a whopping dose of affront and ego, I kept entering each year, with a recipe whose nuance would garner me the accolades I was certain I deserved. At the Merc, my morning scones sold out before noon and my Dirty Chocolate Cake was legendary; I'd made wedding cakes and catered art openings and faculty events—I knew what I was doing. Trouble was, my oeuvre ran toward what more than a few Jimtowners would call "fancy"—a word I hated for its ability to put the lid on anything that wasn't biscuits and gravy or otherwise straight-up flavorless. I'd once entered the annual chili cook-off in Jamestown, an event for which I prepared for three whole days: roasting green chiles and jalapeños, before marinating in tequila and then grilling chicken breasts for what I called Tequila-lime White Lightning Chicken Chili. The name says it all. Of course it didn't win. Instead, it was Nancy Farmer's red chili made with hamburger and spiced with a mix from King Soopers. I'm sure I shot off my mouth. In a moment of bruised pride, I might have said out loud what I was thinking—that the contests like the cook-off and pie affair were a bit of a pearls-before-swine situation—and I'm even more certain that attitude didn't win me any new fans.

So this year, I signed up to judge the pie and cake contest, instead of entering, and together with Karen Z, who loved to eat, and a bunch of town bachelors who loved to eat for free, picked the winning pie: a sour cherry with a just-thick-enough crust more tender and crispy than any I'd ever made. But not before I'd had to practically go hand to hand with Bill, a grizzled local with bad teeth, because he insisted he "didn't like cherry pie and wasn't going to vote for it."

In the end, the pie prevailed.

*　　*　　*

I felt myself moving across summer's surface: the heat, swallows twirling in air, thunderstorms on the mountain, the echo of which followed me to sleep at night. After having been elected to the JAM board, in a meeting where a man turned to me and said, "I'll resign my seat if you'll take it," I persuaded its members and by now my least biggest fan, Hortense, to let me hold a Movie Night at Elysian Fields in August. "Like the drive-in," I said, "without cars." Trouble was, the cost of equipment rental was hefty, more than JAM typically paid for *anything,* so I laid out a plan on how we could raise funds through a raffle, ticket sales, local and business donations, and a cakewalk, where entrants skirted numbers laid in a circle until the music playing stopped and a number was called for one lucky winner, who collected a cake. Of course there was resistance. JAM funds, I was told, were typically reserved for improvements to sound systems and lights, for performances in town. There was more of the who-the hell-does-she-think-she-is? stink in the air, particularly from tepid Hortense.

"We raise money," she said to me flatly, "we don't spend it on entertainment."

The board was divided into entrenched old-timers, people who like Hortense had begun the organization fifteen years before and wanted to preserve "the way things had always been done" and others who didn't want to hold the same two events every year for the next decade. I shook off Hortense's palpable dislike; she was someone who tended not to love ideas that weren't her own. Still, after the board voted to give the event three hundred dollars (an "unprecedented amount," she exclaimed), it was clear she hoped I'd fail to raise the other thousand dollars needed.

And that's all it took. Nothing like a little opposition to focus the mind.

In August, afternoon monsoons rolled in daily and drained the heat from the day with thundershowers that brought sheets of rain or hail, but the skies cleared for Movie Night as about seventy-five people showed up with camp chairs and blankets to the wide-open field bordered by the creek and the canyon wall where the more than hundred-year-old Jamestown cemetery sat. There had been talk by some of the town's more ornery don't-tread-on-me types, who vowed they would not pay to see a movie in their own town park, that they'd sneak across Jim Creek and watch from the line of trees at the edge of the big park, but there was no trouble.

Turns out, the cakewalk was the real star as people lined up to pay five dollars a shot or three tries for ten bucks to win one of fifteen cakes made by town bakers. Kids walked and ran in the dusky light, giggling as the music played, but it was the adults who really got into it. Cameron, a tall, thin man who was tech guy by day and on the fire department on the weekends, skipped around the circle trying to land on the same number each time. Joey, wearing his signature aloha shirt, his head freshly shorn by Heather, who cut nearly everyone's hair in town, paid for three sets of ten-dollar tries because he wanted so bad to win. He was a merry prankster, the gray-haired poster boy for a bygone era. We'd had our differences, but he was a kind, playful man, and in the end when he lost, his clear disappointment inspired me to bake not a cake but his favorite: banana cream pie. I caramelized the coffee-soaked bananas in sugar and whipped twice the amount of cream for the top and delivered it to his house up the street from the Merc. Joey grinned and gave me a burly, back-thumping hug, then walked the pie jauntily to the Merc to share with the boys, many of whom wouldn't pay for anything there but a few beers, some of whom thought my food was too "fancy."

I heard they ate the whole damn thing.

*　　*　　*

A week later, as I laughed and eewed, listening to Oody, who'd called to regale me with the story of another online date—"Oh my god, he was ten years older than he said he was and talked about his four cars as if that made him *sexy*"—a dark fist-sized body dropped from the open attic-like space above the bedroom. I caught the movement first, and then the signature flapping. It was a bat.

"Oh, Jesus," I exhaled into the phone. It was the sudden appearance that gave me a jolt, not the creature itself.

"I have to go," I said. "I've got a situation."

The bat bobbed haphazardly against the beams of the roof as Elvis followed it around the living room, nose stuck in the air, tail wagging. I had no idea how it had gotten in, and although I kinda liked the idea of bats hanging upside down in the space above my bedroom as I slept at night, the last thing I needed was to bump into it on a murky middle-of-the-night trek to the bathroom. Plus, *bat guano*. Opening the front door and propping open the screen, I turned out the lights and held Elvis with me on the couch. The bumping and fluttering continued. To my dog, this was a magnificent game. He sniffed the air and nuzzled my neck excitedly and strained against his harness. Half an hour passed as the house inhaled the night air. The mountain was quiet. Breathing became meditation as the bat twirled overhead. Finally, I retreated to the bedroom, Elvis in tow, and closed the door.

That night, I slept with the front door wide open.

PART III

Home of the Somewhat Feral

Chapter 8

Controlled Burn

I'd long vowed to avoid a town romance because proximity and loneliness pulled strange pairings out of thin air, and left awkward aftermaths across the mountain. Suzie, whose split from Joey ignited a turf war at the Merc, had wagged her finger at me the day she left, saying, "Import your men." She was right: The gene pool was small. No matter who you were, a little Saturday-night-at-the-Merc flirting led to chin wagging all over town by Sunday brunch. All of this attention tended to step on budding romances. But things were far worse when relationships went sour, or someone began comparing your partner's past with your present.

Even marriages were not exempt. Plenty of long-term relationships had gone suddenly bad, but none more notoriously than when the town put on a musical. Twice in its history, Jamestown had mounted original productions that made—owing to the twin elixirs of shared artistic passion and rehearsal beers—strange bedfellows. The result of which was the rearrangement of several unions around town. Singing, it seemed, stirred more than just the soul.

When couples split, their onerous task was to divide not their homes but the town between them. Breakups were hard on everyone as new groups were jigsawed from established circles of friends. Sometimes it was easiest when one-half of the couple simply moved away.

Still, the town had its serial daters, those who tried on love interests and cast them aside like clothes in a pile. Their reputations, along with their conquests, were the stuff of happy hour and party gossip. My jaw-dropping favorite was Lance, who was just thirty when I first met him. He was a tall, thin drink of water with sandy hair and the aloof charm of David Bowie. Not handsome by any stretch of the imagination, or especially interesting—just another guy with a beer in one hand and cigarette in the other standing on the Merc porch. And yet, he managed to pick off the women in town one by one, and each time, from the awkward, all-knees-and-elbows teen who grew into a raven-maned beauty with terrible taste in men to a silver-haired divorcée twenty years his senior, I was shocked. *How did he do it?*

With Sammy, on the other hand, you could see exactly how. She was an athletic woman with snaky brown hair who exuded sex and went through men and women like saucers of delicious cream. A woman so in love with love that she had been married nine times, twice to the same man. She once slid next to me on the dance floor on a Merc Saturday night, spearing me with what were irresistible feline eyes, purring what a good dancer I was as she rubbed her hand provocatively from my shoulder to my hip.

Avoiding romantic imbroglios in Jamestown was a no-brainer. I was too smart, I told myself. So I never thought I'd fall for Jay. But he was the first man to kiss me in over a decade. Perhaps it was all the time I'd spent alone, the months accumulating like dust on my skin. Perhaps it was proximity to Jamestown, a community I was working to love—all those nights at the Merc, watching people try each other on. Perhaps it was that I had so little practice.

Jay, an unlikely prospect, liked jam bands and parties. I listened to NPR and meditated. A gentle, bighearted man with broad shoulders, wild dark hair, and blue eyes, Jay was part deadhead, part Grizzly Adams, and unfailingly sweet.

I knew him from the Merc, where I often pushed him out the door after he'd had one too many beers on my regular Monday night. The shift was perfect for two reasons: It was brief and I was in charge. I opened the café at four, after it had been closed since the previous afternoon, and served not the overly deep-fried and grilled bar menu Joey loved but a quick homey special for which I shopped myself: meat loaf and mashed potatoes, buttermilk fried chicken, chicken tacos. As both cook and waitress, I made good money even when just a handful of people stopped by for dinner or an after-work beer. Best of all, the Merc closed at eight and I was out the door by nine.

Jay was a charming drunk, a bit sappy. Harmless, I thought, as he turned his big blue eyes my way one spring evening and told me I looked nice. I laughed and looked down at my flour-smeared apron and said, "Flattery will get you everywhere, my friend," serving him a beer on the house for which he left a tip equal to the cost of the draw.

I flirted back because of the improbability of it all. There was no way it would go any further. For once, I'd bask in the attention cast my way. As that spring warmed into summer and Monday nights at the Merc moved from boys at the bar to people on the patio, Jay began showing up every week, taking a place at the bar inside to chat me up, leaving big tips while I delivered plates and served drinks outside.

Turns out he lived just a half mile from my house in the basement apartment of a home only seasonally inhabited by its owner. Like me, he walked his dog around the peeper pond. More often, I'd seen him from my kitchen window, as he skirted the edge of my acre lot with Skunk, a black border collie with a white stripe down his back. All along, I'd treated Jay's crush with the mild interest of someone scanning the paper for news, even after he had showed up to shovel my driveway and walk in an improbable deep April snow. Then in July, as I sat grading papers on my deck, I saw Jay strolling down the road, thick arms swinging. He carried himself like a lumberjack wearing leather boots and wool socks, a flannel shirt thrown over a T-shirt. I waved and he waved back, then stopped. Hesitated. And turned up my drive.

Elvis leapt from the deck and raced up to Jay, then went nose to nose with Skunk. The two bobbed and bowed and began chasing.

Jay tromped up the path beneath the aspens.

"Walk?" he said, his big palms spread wide in front of him. Skunk and Elvis raced by, Elvis careening toward the meadow.

"I guess I have no choice," I said, laughing at the dogs.

More walks ensued.

By early August, Jay and I were taking trails deeper and deeper into the woods, walking for an hour at a time, over the Cushman Ranch and sometimes up the St. Vrain, not far from where we lived. We talked a lot about cooking, something Jay loved to do, but like our personalities, our styles were different. Jay liked to make big batches of chili or pasta, even in the summer, and grill huge slabs of meat. I preferred salsas and chutneys with chicken or pork chops, and made blackberry galettes and pizza on the grill.

One day, while we skirted a path around High Lake, tromping along its boggy edges, Jay held out his hand as I stepped over a log. The sudden tenderness of the gesture surprised me. The hand suggested possibility, an invitation. I hesitated. *Oh, what the hell.* I let myself lean into him as I stepped closer. For once, I'd say yes.

Jay asked if he could cook me dinner the next night, another gesture that charmed me. I'm a sucker for someone else in the kitchen. Too often, my not-meat-and-potatoes menus resulted in friends saying they were afraid to cook for me. Like everyone else, I loved being fed.

I spent the whole next day talking myself in and out of what I thought might happen. In the end, I put on a sundress and drank a glass of wine and sat in the early evening listening to the aspens rustle in a mercifully cool breeze. *What harm could a little kissing do?*

Jay arrived with two grocery bags full of food and cooking pans, a six-pack, and two bottles of wine. He produced two different size hotel pans he'd borrowed from Joey at the Merc. In one lay a slab of precooked ribs rubbed with his "special blend," wrapped in foil.

"When did that happen?" I asked, pointing at the ribs.

"For the last four hours," he said, smiling.

Jay got out the smaller hotel pan and a bundle of clams wrapped in paper. He put the pan right on my grill and after seasoning the clams, covered the pan with more foil, vented with slits. We drank a rioja and ate the clams, which were smoky tasting and buttery, while the ribs warmed on the grill. Then we ate the ribs—meat falling off the bone—with a salad I made and licked our fingers as light fell from the day.

Turns out, Jay had spent a long time alone too.

"I'm the happiest lonely guy you'll ever meet," he said, and then fell silent, squinting at me over the rim of his glass.

"What?" I said.

"I just wondered what it would be like to kiss you," he said.

In that moment, I allowed myself to imagine so many things. How easy it was to let go, to follow where the trail led. My last thought as I let curiosity carry me over the cliff was *Of course my romance would be different.*

I was astonished at how fast I shucked my armor as mild interest gave way to giddy delight. It'd been a few years since I'd had a crush, twenty since I'd had a boyfriend. The truth is, early on, I'd decided that falling in love was frivolous. As friends of both sexes pined away for true love, I reckoned that I had far more substantive things to do. By the time I'd figured out that partnership wasn't all bad, I'd far passed the age for the kind of training-wheel education in romance you get in high school and college. To be blunt: When it came to courtship, I was like a five-year-old riding a motorcycle.

For a few weeks as summer pushed into fall, the days passed in a fevered haze. "Let's be happy," Jay said, squeezing my hand and calling me Angel. I accepted each murmured endearment, each declaration of love, each gesture, as something rare and precious. As unexpected as a sudden change in weather.

Jay wanted to "do all the things couples do," and so we packed the ebbing season with firsts: We camped, we flew kites, we ate out, went to concerts, met each other's friends. Falling asleep one night, just weeks into our romance, he called me the love of his life.

"When are you two moving in?" Joey asked one morning at the Merc. I shook my head and made a face, but there was part of me that wanted to simply surrender. *Sure,* I thought, *let's.* I was tired of being careful. When it came to people, I'd held myself at bay for so long, convinced I wasn't cut out for closeness.

My friend Rainbow, a thirty-something cook at the Merc who'd just finished her graduate degree and was my ally in a mutual quest to get Joey to serve better food, cheered my romance from the start.

"Stop thinking," she said, "just do it."

When, a few months after graduation, she found out she was pregnant, she looked at me half-resigned, half-hopeful, and shook her wavy locks.

"I wish you were having a baby too," she said.

At first I laughed. Her suggestion was ridiculous. Of course Jay and I wouldn't have a baby. From the start there were signs that this romance would not last, but I ignored them, drunk on proximity and contact, delirious at having someone who held my hand.

Too soon, our differences pushed between us.

In late September, Jay and I attended a wedding together, the first such event for me since Elvis had been my date at my sister's wedding, a part hippie, part death-metal affair to which I wore black harness boots and Elvis wore a tie with a trout on it. Jay's longtime buddy was marrying his longtime girlfriend in a mountain aspen grove in what turned out to be the first snow of the season. When the pastor asked the couple if they promised to be "friends, lovers, and partners" for life, Jay tenderly whispered the phrase in my ear and squeezed my hand. Neither of us could know that the marriage would be over in less than a year.

It was chilly outside, and gold leaves stuck to everyone's shoes. Afterward, Jay showed me off, introducing me to more people than I could remember, before abruptly leaving me for thirty-minute intervals while he snorted lines of coke with the groomsmen. By the time we left, I couldn't get warm; my face and hands were red with cold. On the long drive home, as snow pelted the highway, I said something about the trouble of having an outdoor mountain wedding without a backup, imagining the last-minute scuffle to rent and erect a party tent, trying not to think or talk about Jay's now-you-see-me-now-you-don't behavior. I felt a familiar brick lodged in my chest. I was pissed.

In response, Jay shook his head.

"It was all her," he said, meaning Shawna, the bride. "She insisted on being married in the aspens. I told Derek, 'It's her day, let her do what she wants. If she wants to ride a zebra and wear a crown, then let her. She's been dreaming of this every single day since she was a little girl.'"

"What do you mean?" I forced a laugh. "Dreaming of what?"

"Her wedding day." Jay looked at me earnestly.

"Are you kidding?" I said. "Who thinks that anymore?"

"It's the most important day in a woman's life."

"Oh my god." I groaned and then was silent.

When we pulled into my driveway, I let him have it.

I was furious, I said, that I'd been carted to an event where I knew no one and left to make small talk with strangers. Jay said I needed "to relax" because everyone "loved me" and thought I was "sweet," an adjective that simply did not circle my orbit.

"You can go now," I said, getting out of the car.

The next day we put plaster on the wound. I ignored Jay's ideas about marriage and he apologized for leaving me alone. In the following weeks, Jay stayed in Boulder after work more often to hang out with his friends at the bar and then announced he wanted to see me only on weekends.

"I have a lot to do," he said. He preferred sleeping in his own bed.

I put up with it for a while, honestly reluctant to give up the luxury of holding on to a body at night instead of a wad of pillows. I also came to like the town's softened reaction to me. When they saw Jay and me holding hands, I suddenly became visible. Invitations were extended from couples with whom I'd been on friendly hi-how-ya-doing? terms: "We have to have *you two* for dinner." Bob the Brit, one of the Merc drunks, bought me a beer one night as "an apology" because, he sheepishly confessed, he'd thought I "liked girls." Even Joey was a whole lot nicer, raving about how happy he was for me—as if he'd finally figured me out, relieved I wasn't as threatening or sharp as he'd thought I was. Now whenever I saw him, he wrapped me in a bear hug.

A few weeks later, I got my finger lodged in the hydraulic wood splitter as I tried to power through an entire cord of wood—alone, in a single day. I'd asked Jay for help, but he'd responded that he had plans. I was moving fast, automatically shoving wood onto the metal beam with my left hand while pulling the lever of the splitter with my right. Suddenly I felt pressure on my left middle finger, which I had absentmindedly dangled along the back of the splitting brace, and now the finger was lodged between it and a pine log. For a long breathless second, I panicked, trying to pull my finger free as the pressure steadily increased. Then I realized my right hand was controlling the anvil of the splitter against the log and I thrust the lever in the opposite direction. My finger emerged, flattened like a deflated balloon, a small fissure running the length between the nail bed and the knuckle. I ran inside and quickly wrapped it in a towel and put some ice on it. *Fuck,* I thought. It was Sunday. The cost of an ER visit would empty my savings, the sum saved for this season's snow tires. My brain buzzed over my options, my finger throbbed.

I refused to call Jay. Instead, I called Judith, who wasn't home, and then Karen Z.

"Don't look at it," she said, and hung up. She was at my door ten minutes later armed with a pint of bourbon, a brand-new, tags-still-on first aid kit, and a bag of frozen peas.

"When did you get this?" I asked, as she cut the zip tie that held the bag closed. Karen shrugged. "Who knows."

She dug out gauze and tape and disinfectant while I took a slug from the bottle and unwrapped my finger. It stung in the air but had regained some of its former shape. I could move it. Carefully, I prodded the skin back into place and Karen dotted the cut with Mercurochrome. We taped it together with a butterfly bandage and then I wrapped it in gauze and taped the finger to my pointer, placing the bag of peas on top of it. We toasted with more bourbon.

"Good thing," I said.

"Yeah," said Karen, and then told me the story of Bonnie, a friend who had chopped off the tip of her finger splitting wood. By the time she'd wrapped it in a towel and drove herself to the emergency room, "it was too late."

Jay dropped by hours later with a first aid kit and some chocolate, sweetly apologetic. Still, after making sure I was fine, he left.

The finger broke in earnest two weeks later when my hand slipped opening the latch on my truck door, and a knife blade of pain shot through the digit. An X-ray confirmed the fracture. It was still splinted when Jay and I attended another wedding in November. We'd been tilting along, making hopeful plans to host a Thanksgiving dinner at my house. "Let's get through the holidays and then regroup," said Jay, after another squabble. At the time, it sounded sensible, not desperate. Neither of us had ever spent Christmas with someone.

The wedding, for Divya and Damadar, my yoga instructor and her longtime boyfriend, was at the Hare Krishna temple in Denver. We arrived late, a full thirty minutes into the ceremony, because I'd copied the MapQuest directions wrong and we'd zigzagged all over. Jay insisted he could find the way by systematically cruising the streets in search of a combination of block and street numbers while I wanted to go back and start over where we got off track. We argued.

Inside the gold-domed building, we removed our shoes and stood in the doorway to the ceremonial hall, unable to enter. Jay was clearly uncomfortable. He'd made a few Hare Krishna jokes on the drive down and I'd snapped at him.

"Stop being such a conservative; it's not a cult."

The pashmina-ed and sari-clad audience was assembled on blue pillows on the floor, in front of an altar. The bride and groom sat in the center, along with a pundit in a white dhoti, around a square fire pit. There were offerings of fruit and sesame seeds and ghee on silver platters. Rose-scented incense filled the air. We'd only missed the tying-the-knot ceremony, where the couple fasten their garments together as a symbol of their union and commitment and then remain that way for three whole days as a reminder of their bond.

After the pundit chanted his blessing for the new union, Divya and Damadar fed the ceremonial fire with fruit and sesame seeds as the pundit told the audience that "loving means sacrifice." More smoke filled the room. Jay stood behind me the whole time, in a tight black dress shirt he'd bought for the occasion, hands on my shoulders, as if pressing me back to earth.

Afterward, I watched the newlyweds walk around greeting guests. Divya was pulling Damadar by the hand from place to place, the shawl that connected them tied in a huge, heavy knot. He was a sweet man who attended Divya's all-women's yoga class on Sundays. No matter what she said to Damadar in the blunt style she reserved for him only—"Not like that! You'll ruin your ankles!"—he smiled serenely. His calm, devotional love impressed me. Now he followed in her footsteps.

"That's their relationship," I said to Jay, nodding at the couple, "but he doesn't seem to mind."

Afterward, Jay didn't spend the night. We'd stopped at a bar because the wedding was a nonalcoholic affair and Jay needed a drink. I sipped a glass of wine while he downed three bourbon and Cokes and chatted with the bartender, ignoring me.

I said nothing.

The next day, as we skirted the peeper pond with the dogs, Jay said, "We have to end this." I don't know why I was stunned. I walked beside him, silent, watching the dried summer grass bend and shift. It was one of those cloudy fall days that smelled like winter. A cold wind blew.

"Why?" I finally asked when we returned to my cabin.

"I'm just not ready," he said.

There was a moment after Divya and Damadar's wedding when the Lord Krishna was revealed, and bride and groom, along with the temple members, fervently prostrated themselves before the blue-skinned god. Watching their devotion, I was moved to think we should all sacrifice to those things that are bigger than us, to make room for the divine and the miraculous. That's what I thought I had been doing with Jay, when instead I'd fallen for the trappings—for the ritual—not the god. Our mutual yearning wasn't strong enough glue to make us stick; our romance could never hold the weight of a possible future.

*   *   *

As fall deepened in earnest and snow pummeled the mountain, the Forest Service burned slash piles in the steep valley between Jamestown and Overland Mountain. I drove home from my Merc Monday night watching the eerie shadow of flames burning between trees—bonfires spilling across the valley. Absent the artificial glow of the city, nights were normally inky, lit not by streetlights but stars. Now over a dozen fires burned in the dark valley, casting shadowy, surreal light. Wind-racked tree limbs shook and wavered, their movements shape-shifting each fire, making it look monstrous.

Any light source in the darkened windy landscape—whether it was a campfire or the glow cast by a winter-lit home, even the rising moon—appeared spectral, any illumination like the vivid burning edge of flames. Too often, I'd mistaken the radiance of my neighbor's enormous spotlight on the forested hill to the west for fire as I stood at the window near the kitchen table a hundred yards away and worried the shifting light between trees meant a blaze caused by downed electrical lines, the origin of the Overland fire near Jamestown four years back. I'd even gotten dressed in the middle of the night a couple of times and driven over to check for myself because the thought of flames left me sleepless.

That night, passing those fires, I was breathless, sure their obscured flickering coupled with sharp gusts of wind meant they were, or would soon be, out of control. At home, I called the county dispatch, but the operator informed me the burns were "controlled."

For a few seasons now, the Forest Service had been thinning trees, collecting the chain-sawed sections in large piles across remote draws up and down the valley and scattered across the mountain between Jamestown and my cabin. Last summer, they'd cut huge road-like swaths through the woods, across some of the trails Jay and I took, in an effort to put space between trees and prevent crown fires—where fast-moving flames leapt from the top of one tree to the next. The downed wood was added to the existing cairns dotting the landscape, some fifteen feet in diameter, and now the heaps were being lit, a few dozen at a time. What made it "safe" was that the air temperatures were frigid and the ground frozen. Still, a crazy wind raked the valley. The fires swirled and banked, shifting with wind.

Of course I couldn't sleep. Every gust of wind sent my heart crashing against my chest. *What if they were wrong?* I imagined the fire rushing up-canyon over the top of the mountain, pressing toward the cabin, a tidal wave of flame. In between breaths, I plotted how much I could grab—dog, computer, photos—as I flew out the door to my truck, racing south over an undulating dirt road toward the Peak to Peak Highway, the only available escape route. Although it had been more than three years since my cabin had burned, I often dreamed about fleeing fire. In these dreams, an inferno marched over the mountain like an army extending as far as the eye could see in one incendiary line, or smoke clogged the air, obscuring the cabin like thick mist as I searched for a way out or tried to reach Elvis, who was home alone.

The next morning, smoke rose from the mounds filling the valley as I descended in the early light to teach a class at the community college. A darkened haze mingled with tendrils of clouds moving up-canyon. The landscape was already winter bleak—just snow and browned-out patches between pines. Ash blew from the still-glowing mouths of more than two dozen slash piles along steep slopes; it looked like the aftermath of war, like Armageddon. I pulled the truck over and gazed out across the valley, watching early-morning crows as smoke and clouds obscured the sun.

By that evening, the Forest Service had posted signs announcing: CONTROLLED BURN: PLEASE DO NOT REPORT. The fires were safe, they insisted. Folks on the mountain had flooded the dispatch with calls the night before. We'd all seen it too many times: a prescribed burn that jumped its lines, fire that refused to behave. I drove uneasily up and down the valley for the next two weeks, as new piles were lit and others continued to smolder. Smoke lingered in the air like memory, casting a haze over the valley.

* * *

On Christmas morning, five weeks after Jay and I broke up, I made coffee in my French press and watched the snow fall outside, writing an email to Oody, who was planning a visit in the summer. Elvis sat beside me on the couch.

Oody had written a poem called "Kissing Elvis" after she slid into my pickup on a rainy Milwaukee night, saying, "Hello, handsome," and Elvis caught her open mouth with his full tongue.

"If I'd closed my eyes," she joked, "it might have been the best kiss I ever had."

Remember that? I wrote.

The last time she'd visited, I was living in the horse barn in Left Hand Canyon writing my dissertation and she was passing through with her boyfriend, a soft-spoken man with wavy dark blond hair, on their way to Taos. They had stayed in a B and B in the canyon and we'd gone to the Merc for Suzie's brunch and drunk too many mimosas. That boyfriend was long gone, but Oody had admirably been outfitted with lovers over the years. Until recently, her dating life had been my one curbside thrill. Last summer, I'd returned the favor. After a week with Jay, I wrote to her: *What have I done all these years without kissing?*

Being alone felt different now. It wasn't Jay that I missed but human touch.

I'd planned another solitary Christmas, declining invitations to be with happy couples in favor of some good old-fashioned wound licking. I would spend the day snacking on what my grandfather had called "deli lunch," a platter of meat and cheese—prosciutto and salami with Maytag blue cheese, Brillat-Savarin, and an aged Gouda. I had good bread and olives and chicken liver pâté, along with figs and grapes and a chewy petite Syrah. I planned to spend the whole day, after a walk with Elvis, watching the BBC's *Pride and Prejudice* with Colin Firth.

But the sky had barely brightened from pink to blue when a car appeared in the drive and out climbed Judith and David.

"Merry Christmas!" they sang from the driveway as I opened the door and Elvis bounded excitedly down the steps and out to meet them. I hadn't expected to see them—they celebrated the solstice with a party for friends. "On Christmas," she told me, "we get the children one big present each," something they asked for months in advance, "and then we play games or take a walk." She grinned. "I don't cook and the day is blessedly without expectation."

David carried a huge piece of wood up the steps and presented it to me.

"Your Yule log, m'lady." It was from an apple tree that broke during a storm.

"We brought champagne and breakfast," Judith announced.

I put the log in the stove and left the doors open so we could smell its sweet scent and then put out green glass plates and flutes for the champagne. We toasted each other over a plate of scones Judith's daughter, Ryan, had made, along with Judith's homemade lemon curd and some creamy and expensive European butter. The family lived frugally, but Judith managed to eke out luxurious touches.

I served reheated slices of an apple and cinnamon galette I'd made the day before and we sat at the table near the wall pine I'd decorated with white Christmas lights as Elvis settled at my feet.

Judith presented me with a series of cards she'd made by cutting out pictures and pasting them together.

"These things remind me of you." One card had a sunflower and a bee, another had the moon and thousands of stars. The last had a woman standing on a mountain with her arms thrust up at the sky. Beneath her, inside the mountain, slept a bear curled in a den.

"And this too," she said, handing me a wad of tissue hiding a toy silver tiara with pink plastic stones. My favorite color. I laughed.

"I have always wanted one of these," I said, putting on the tiara. "It's good to be the queen."

There were also jars of Judith's Italian plum jam and mango chutney.

The kids sent handmade candles, and David gave me a pink lotus flower that held a small votive.

Before they left, David shoveled the walk as Judith and I refilled the wood box.

"Merry Christmas, darling," she said, kissing me goodbye.

As snow began falling all over again, the day lightened immeasurably.

Chapter 9

Home of the Somewhat Feral

I couldn't remember so much snow. No winter had seemed so full, so much like what winter should be. Just after Christmas, weekly storms backed into the mountain, unloading over a foot at a time. While a mere eight inches was enough to close schools in Boulder County, snows on Overland routinely tripled that amount. I'd spend an hour digging out and then drive down-canyon, watching the snow level plummet over the course of the fourteen-mile and three-thousand-foot descent. In Boulder, a mere dusting. On days when I had to teach a class at the college, I left the house clad in lug-soled Bearpaws, a hat, and my woolie, tossing a leather coat and my too-slick-for-snow harness boots or an even less sensible pair of ankle boots with spiked heels into the truck seat along with my books.

By the third week of January, my deck was a raft in a swell of snow. The path to the truck was hip deep. Elvis, who was twelve and had been with me for eleven years still managed to make a game of burying his face in snow, but now his trail skirted the edges of the bigger banks piled in the yard. He'd begun using the cleared path to relieve himself rather than climb to his normal spot on the berm.

With too much winter at my door, I tried to imagine the opposite end of the year. On days when the snow shivered out of the sky and the stove ticked with burning wood, it was impossible to remember open windows and flowers and sleeveless mornings in the garden. Equally impossible was conjuring leafless aspens and a landscape iced over beneath deep pockets of snow while the grasses were thigh high and the meadows churned out wildflowers. From either end of the year, I could not quite believe its opposite ever existed. It was like trying to remember love, how happy I was with Jay for a brief few weeks before winter. I could no longer summon the sense that all was right with the world that I'd had for a scant moment with him—that jolt of everything being deliciously as it should be—but like charming, ephemeral summer, I knew it was beautiful.

Into this landscape roared the winter wind. After each snow, days of it. Forty-, fifty-, sixty-mile-an-hour gusts sent sheets of white scudding across my driveway and the meadows, remaking the landscape. At night, it pounded the cabin with bursts that made the wood two-by-four walls creak and sent winter-laden limbs crashing down from above. Wind so loud, so unrelenting, I pulled out my summer fan and put it on high, aiming it at the wall in the bedroom to drown out the freight train roaring off the divide during the night.

Despite the snow fence, the woodpile needed daily excavation. I plowed my 4Runner back and forth through drifts in the morning and at night to keep my driveway open and avoid calling one of the local snow removal guys because the repeated cost in such relentless weather might just break the bank.

In the meantime, I went hand to hand with the county plow operator, who had a habit of blocking in my driveway on his rounds to clear the road. I'd no sooner shovel myself out than he'd come by and bury the entrance to my drive with four feet of heavy, crusted crap. I had been shoveling and shoveling. My back hurt all the time. Hauling wood in the postal crates was grueling, and I was crabby from too much wind.

The next time I heard the *beep beep* of the plow from the dreamy distance of a winter nap, I leapt from bed, grabbed my shovel, and raced to the mouth of my drive. He already had me half blocked in. I could hear his progress around the loop as he backed and scraped, backed and scraped, while I scooped snow out into the street. When he neared, I stood in the street, shoving heavy clumps over my shoulder, my back to him. He honked. I kept shoveling, head down. He stopped and then honked again. I stepped slightly back, a bit to the side of the pile, as he moved forward slowly, angling the middle blade on the tractor in a scalloping fashion, and cut the snow away from the drive. The blade pruned a pile just two feet from my toes. This time when he backed up, I moved and he widened my driveway.

Thank you, I mouthed as he drove away.

During one storm, the wind raged across the hours and minutes of three long days. I couldn't see out to the road. I couldn't walk the dog. Most annoyingly, I could not go out unless outfitted like someone on a polar expedition. I wore ski goggles against the needling flakes. When finally the sky opened blue and clear, the trees flocked in winter white by an arctic mass that descended and chased the wind away, I sat happily listening to nothing, relieved. Suddenly, the power, out for more than a day, roared back on. Every light in the house ignited abruptly, startling me as I boiled water for coffee on the iron top of the woodstove. The sound of the refrigerator humming to life was a car engine in a barren landscape.

After a few seasons up on the mountain, I was well prepared for the routine power outages of winter. I had stashed candles, head-lamps hanging on the knobs of the front door and my bedroom, a couple of jugs of drinking water, and most important, an already ground stash of coffee in the freezer. The well reserve tank held three or four flushes if I wasn't doing dishes, so I used them judi-ciously. I could melt snow on top of the stove, if needed, where I could also warm leftovers wrapped in a bit of foil. Or I pulled out my one-burner and made something on the deck outside.

Snow scalloped my windows with over a foot of powder on the west and east sides of the house, and the eastern loop of the cul-de-sac was completely impassable, blocked by a twelve-foot-high drift that stretched thirty feet. I tiptoed halfway up before miserably post-holing down as Elvis easily trotted to the top and leaned over the edge. The look on his face was intrepid—the great explorer and discoverer of new lands.

"Careful," I called. I was more nervous about his love of edges now that he was older. He turned and cantered down and out into the road, bunny-hopping ahead. His legs weren't what they used to be, his hearing going too. I'd first noticed it on windy days at the peeper pond, when he cantered ahead. I shouted over the riffling air. Nothing. Then, louder. *He's getting old,* I thought, waving and walking faster to catch his attention.

We took the road back to the cabin, traversing the drifts in the driveway—three- and four-foot swells—too much for my truck to plow down. Buddy, who'd stopped by the Merc the night before for my Basque beef stew, offered to plow my drive for "some baking." I stomped my boots at the cabin door and carried them to the hearth to dry, then pulled out an extra-large Bundt pan and measured flour, butter, and powdered sugar for an orange cranberry pecan pound cake and waited for Buddy and his backhoe.

*   *   *

As February rolled into view, I talked Joey into letting me host a JAM Poetry Night on Valentine's Day—partly because I saw it as my duty as the new vice president of JAM (Hortense had been ousted in our January meeting in the small-town equivalent of a bloodless coup) to continue to push the organization past its pickin' and singin' ethos and partly because if I had a superpower, it would be to cultivate poetry lovers everywhere.

At first Joey was resistant. Valentine's would fall on a night when the regulars were mostly guys drinking beer.

"No one cares about that," he said, dismissing me. "They won't come."

"They will if you make spaghetti."

I'll admit I was flattering him. Whenever Joey served his special, people packed the Merc, greedy for a plate of what one Merc cook had accurately described as "a Bloody Mary with frozen meatballs and sausages bouncing to the top instead of ice cubes." The mysterious concoction always sold out.

"I'll make Dirty Chocolate Cake," I offered. The cake was fast and altitude-proof, "dirty" because the secret ingredient was mayonnaise.

"Come on, Joey, Jamestown needs our love."

When he finally agreed, I made flyers that said FEEL THE LOVE and announced the event on the QT, promising bawdy, funny, and silly alternatives to sappy love poems. Whether single, coupled, or love-averse, I said, all could participate.

My tradition of mocking Valentine's Day began in grad school at CU when, weary of the spectacle made at the retail store where I worked, I announced I was sick of crappy love poems and candy hearts. In protest, I hosted a dinner for Lucia and Elizabeth—all of us single, all a bit too sharp at the edges, all wearing nineties burgundy lipstick. I pulled a café table into the living room of the Bow Mountain house and lit candles and served pasta puttanesca, an appropriately prickly dish with anchovies and capers and black olives. We read dark and bruising poems about love, like Luis Urrea's "Man's Fate," in which the speaker talks about the things he does when his lover leaves ("Crap with the door open," "Defiant beer"), and laughed and laughed, feeling above it all. Then Lucia, who had been married three times before she was thirty, pulled out a tender poem about kisses, reading it in her soft, velvety voice.

"Oh," I said. "Who is that?"

"Ed," said Lucia, smiling. Ed Dorn, the capricious head of the writing program and Lucia's good friend, was a poet whose later work was, like Ed himself, a howl of sarcasm and despair. As I served heart-shaped chocolate tarts with raspberries, I tried to link the man I knew to the delicate syllables on the page. Beneath his legendary scowl lay some tenderness.

At the Merc, my plot was to engage Joey's gang of grizzled bachelors—"the boys," Karen Z and I called them. Some, I hoped, might be closet poetry lovers. So, I printed three dozen of the most quirky and nontraditional love poems I could find—everything from Kate Braverman's incantatory hallucinations about madness and steamy sex to William Carlos Williams' quiet evocation of desire over plums—and carted my pages along with three bags of poetry books and anthologies to the Merc and spread them out on a table. There would be something for everyone. Anyone could walk in, pick out a poem, and read it aloud. Even the unprepared could get in on the action, and as an added bonus, the audience wouldn't be dulled to a halt listening to too many would-be poets.

I poured a glass of wine from behind the bar while Joey gleefully doled out plates of pasta, gathering compliments by the fistful, and greeting everyone with his "Hiya!" as if he were the mayor of the town.

When enough bodies had stuffed themselves near the dark bar at the rear of the Merc, and the wood tables were more than half-full of the curious and the hungry—about thirty people in all—I began circulating poetry books, handing them out like a gypsy telling fortunes.

"Read this one," I said to Jovan, a man who wore a bowler hat and blinked too much, passing him a volume by Russell Edson, the connoisseur of quirky.

"You might like Billy Collins," I said to Hollis, a confirmed bachelor and auto mechanic (in that order) who had legendarily rebuffed every single come-on leveled his way, opening the book to "Victoria's Secret," a poem about a man distracted by the sexy catalog full of lingerie-clad women looking at him.

One by one people signed up to read—at first, the die-hard poetry lovers.

Judith read her favorite poem by Kathleen Raine, which repeats the phrase "because I love" over and over, and I read Robert Hass' "Privilege of Being," which I'd once seen deployed in the most erotic way by a slinky poet named Simone on a room full of breathless men and women. The poem is full of a kind of voluptuous emptiness and existential longing, but it worked for Simone, whom I later saw straddling the thighs of a muscular young man. The power of poetry.

As the evening continued, the words of a few Romantic poets were uttered, along with a passage from *Tristan and Isolde*. Then one of the boys, a man called Snake Habenero, who played the banjo and road his dirt bike to the Merc in the summertime, stepped up to the mic. By looks, he was easy to dismiss—a bit of a drunkard with a wild gray beard and hair that curled out in thick tendrils from under his cap. He wore wire-rimmed glasses, a year-round Hawaiian shirt—but he was as smart as he was genial. Well read, a connoisseur of movies. With his reddened and puffy hands shoved into his jean pockets, he opened his mouth to recite "The Shooting of Dan McGrew" from memory as the beer drinkers at the bar whooped and hollered.

That's all it took.

One by one, the boys at the back cut themselves from the herd and moseyed across the painted pinewood floor to the mic, standing in an alcove framed by the front window strung with multicolored teardrop-shaped lights beneath the gold- and red-painted words JAMESTOWN MERCANTILE CAFE.

Louie read the poem I'd handed to Hollis and Chad read one by Emily Dickinson. Jimmy, who spoke five languages, read a poem in French. But the showstopper was Kent—a man with an unmistakable, grizzled voice, whose gray beard was always neat, his thick hair combed straight back. He shared his house on the hill across from the Merc with a rotating cast of bachelors. There was a pool table and a hot tub and big-screen TV. There was always beer.

Earlier, I had handed him a book of Charles Bukowski poems as he sat on his stool drinking Joey's cheapest beer.

"These are right up your alley," I said.

As Kent stood up and walked to the mic, the guys at the bar whistled and clapped. Everyone looked up from their plates. Joey yelled "Kent!" in encouragement.

"To love," said Kent, raising his Budweiser, and read a poem about sex and eating. Instead of the word *cunt,* he said *vagina,* pronouncing it "vajeen," with a soft French *j,* drawing out the syllables so that they trailed off like a whisper. I couldn't tell if he was embarrassed or trying to spare the fainter of heart. There was a moment of stunned silence as he uttered the word, a bit of shock, and then the room erupted in howls of laughter as Kent continued to growl out the words of the poem with a caginess that was equal parts impudence and reserve.

The Merc had had its share of legendary nights, nights when folks got up on tables and danced, and the chandeliers swung back and forth over a crowd of sweating, out-of-control bodies. Some nights, things were broken—the front window at least twice—or a scuffle broke out. And the next day, the talk in town elevated what had happened in people's minds so that the story would be told and told again. Mostly, these nights revolved around drinking and music, and the urges each releases. That night, it was just poetry. And like all legendary Jamestown nights, people still talk about it—the night Kent read a poem at the Merc.

*   *   *

Jamestown had always prided itself on being "Home of the Somewhat Feral"—a phrase emblazoned on the handwritten Merc menu. Locals felt some pride concerning their wilder natures, and for this reason, they considered themselves cut from different cloth than flatlanders. This meant the town attracted its share of miscreants, in addition to the usual batch of loners and libertarians. On one or two occasions, there was someone so crazy, the town banded together to gently urge relocation. But typically, trouble came in two forms: the drunk and the young and indolent.

Every spring, a new crowd of hippie-wannabes showed up, kids in their early twenties—women in dreads, men in beards—dressed in layer upon layer of mismatching clothes. By fall, most had moved on because the "Sugar Magnolia" fantasy of lazy days of music and rent-free living ground to a halt with the first deep snow.

That year it got bad, fueled in no small part by a new hippie chick in the Merc kitchen who, sorry for the hungry masses, slipped free food and beer to the latest arrivals. Two arrived, then two weeks later, two more, followed by a group of four and a few others. They had a grapevine going: *In Jamestown, the livin' was easy.*

Fed up with the patio full of freeloaders who guzzled Joey's beer all spring and created clouds of fuck-you smoke in front of the Merc, I flyered the post office, the fire department bulletin board, and the Merc with posters promoting California's Black Bear Commune, whose "free land for free people" had been a sixties anthem. Over an image of a groovy-looking group of people holding hands in a circle in a forested clearing I'd found on the group's website, I wrote: "Wanted: Free People Who Want to Live Free on Free Land Forever." Beneath the image I provided information on the commune and its rich history, and gave directions.

It probably didn't have much to do with my flyers, but by late summer, the town belonged to the locals again.

Besides we had our own brand of freeloaders, locals who treated the Merc like their own living room, grabbing cigarette packs from beneath the cash register counter and helping themselves to refills of beer. Sometimes not paying. People who turned down the lights or changed the music without asking, who never once ordered so much as a cup of coffee, or who brought their own beer tucked inside a paper bag. Since the business relied heavily on local patronage to stay afloat—especially in winter—these transgressions always burned my butt and made me impatient with the worst offenders.

More onerous was the fact that the Merc had a history of letting people put their food on a tab. You were supposed to plunk down a hundred dollars and then use it as credit when you came in, but the practice fell by the wayside under Joey's reign, and "The Book" was now a three-inch-thick binder of IOUs. A conservative estimate put the total owed to Joey at well over five thousand dollars, but I'd bet it was more like ten. People from the surrounding mountain towns of Gold Hill and Ward had pages. So did friends of friends, people from Boulder and beyond. It was hard to keep track of everyone.

In small towns, trust and cooperation were the unspoken currency. But for some reason there were more than a few who felt honestly justified in stiffing the Merc, as if the business that had operated as a combination of the town's communication center, beating heart, and therapy couch for decades *owed them*. People who took advantage of the safety net the Merc generously offered: Out of milk and eggs and money on a snowy day? In need of a quick McMerc and cup of coffee on the way down-canyon? Or a bottle of wine forgotten in the list of errands, going up-canyon? The Merc provided.

*   *   *

JAM's new president was DJ, a bassist and soundman, playwright and director, who like me, wanted to see JAM diversify; our plan was to host one event each month. In March it was Band in a Hat, a JAM tradition, whose motto was "Dare to Suck." We added a taco bar and hat contest; Joey kept the Merc open for beer, and the night exploded into a bacchanal when the town's professional soprano sang "Touch-a, touch-a, touch me, I wanna be dirty" and Jerry, one of the boys, played off-beat tambourine as one band's go-go girl. In April, it was Karaoke Night at the Merc, another affair that was well lubricated, followed by another poetry night in May, this one dedicated to spring and "mudlusciousness." In June, DJ and I dreamed up something called JavaJAM-A-Palooza, a reimagining of JAM's oldest tradition, JavaJAM. Our idea was to create a daylong festival of the arts in Jamestown. So in addition to an evening of acoustic music and desserts, there would be an art exhibit, performance and spoken-word events, along with cash prizes to encourage even the most reclusive artists to come out.

The whole thing took two days to set up as DJ and I and a handful of JAM volunteers ran back and forth between the park, the town hall, and the JAM office hauling stage pieces and pop-ups, hanging artwork, fixing snafus, and posting flyers and the schedule of events. We ushered judges back and forth, wrangled performers, made announcements, filled in for missing volunteers, and directed people to whatever event was happening now. A bit of an uproar ensued when the art juror we'd procured from CU's art department chose an entry painted by a ten-year-old in town as the winner of the fifty-dollar prize. In the end, the palooza part was fun but exhausting—a bit like throwing a fantastic dinner party that every-one but the host enjoyed.

By July, it was clear our ambition o'erleapt our stamina. The increased activities made most of our core membership—about six or eight people—cranky. DJ and I, who had directed, supported, labored, or cheered on every single event, were out of gas. Snarki-ness and infighting ensued as ruffled feathers fanned more squabbles about new ways and old ways of doing things. People were accused of having agendas. The manner and method of Hortense's exit was a sore spot for one or two. Even DJ and I were weary of each other. We canceled meetings for a couple of months and took the rest of the summer to recharge.

In August, Oody arrived. For once, I fretted over my cabin, with its unfinished walls and pine-branch toilet paper holder. I'd put up large framed mirrors on almost every wall to cover the dark wood and reflect light inside. A few years back I'd installed double-paned windows salvaged from a construction site. Judith had helped me pick colors and paint the kitchen wall red and the tall, thin panel of exposed drywall in the living room a shade of creamy leather. I'd made the cabin cozy, but it was still rustic. Mice ran in and out, there were holes in the screen door. Oody was the most bohemian person I knew: She had lived in a California commune in the sixties and told a story about dropping acid and walking out into the desert, only to return hours later after walking barefoot on the sand, sunburned, and having lost her clothes. Nearly forty years later, she was the fussiest of travelers. I'd mocked her endlessly whenever we'd gone to writing conferences and she unloaded her own pillow along with earplugs, a wineglass, and bag of Cheerios and sugar, the last of which she insisted must be eaten within thirty minutes of waking. I promised to let her have my bed and bought Cheerios and white sugar and juicing oranges for her morning ritual.

I bought a blow-up mattress and dusted every open surface before I descended into the cloudless heat of the Front Range to the airport on the eastern outskirts of Denver to pick up my old friend. Everything about Oody was thin and chic—a hint of Audrey Hepburn without the cold air of propriety and ladylikeness. She had dark hair that curled in clouds before spilling in a collection of corkscrews and spirals out onto her chest. She looked forty-five and had since I'd met her. From the curb, she grinned, wearing her signature red lipstick, and waved, dressed in black jackboots and black jeans, standing next to an oversized suitcase. Shockingly, her black hair now hung in short, straight sheets against her face. Less Audrey Hepburn, more Joan Jett.

"What did you do?" I exclaimed.

"I needed a change," she said. I'd never seen her with short hair.

"Hello, Elvis, my love," she whispered seductively as Elvis stepped between the front seats to lick her face.

Oody and I spent the evening on the deck with Judith. I have never been a huge collector of friends, preferring instead to cultivate a handful of deep connections. I had a fondness for earthy, headstrong women: the bedrock of the world. That night I am certain we could have been mistaken for Macbeth's witches as we cackled and conspired, gleefully telling stories over pinot grigio chilled with frozen strawberries. Judith and Oody shared cigarettes as the shadows drew out across the yard and I grilled shrimp marinated in tequila. Talk turned to the things we couldn't do without.

"My garden," said Judith.

"That," I said, pointing at the barely there view of Indian Peaks, "the quiet. Elvis."

"Wine!" shouted Oody, and we clinked our glasses together.

In the morning, Oody and I sat on the deck and listened to the hummingbirds. The breeze through aspen and pine sounded like water rushing in a stream. Fat clouds puffed by.

"This place is perfect," she said.

Later that day, we hiked the St. Vrain with Elvis and drove across the scenic Peak to Peak between Nederland and Estes Park, but our big event was slated for Saturday night, when Jamestown's one and only punk band, the Measles, would play at the Merc. Fronted by Blake, a prematurely gray lawyer cum musician who was something of a walking music library, the band was part punk education, part noise.

The Merc was packed. I had to muscle my way to the back to get a beer for me and wine for Oody. After Blake's long-winded and slightly academic introduction, the band, dressed in leather and white T-shirts and black eyeliner, roared into the first song and the crowd instantly began to jump and shove. Oody and I joined in.

At first the atmosphere was playful; people pogoed and shook, but then the band launched into "Anarchy in the U.K." and suddenly, elbows and bodies were flying. I got shoved into a table as Oody hastily waved at me and retreated outside for a smoke. Turning, I saw Bob the Brit coming at me with the full force of his body, and I lowered my shoulder and crashed into him. After that I was pushing and jumping and yelling "Fuck you!" at the top of my lungs. It was as if all the times I'd been annoyed by the Merc, the town drunks and horseshoe players who clogged up the park on every single sunny day with a party, the cliquey we've-been-here-longer-than-you residents, had been rolled up into that moment as I kicked and shoved my way through the crowd.

It was fun.

Generally, I avoided violence—the watching of it and the doing of it—not because of some prissy passivity but because I enjoyed it too much. I was uncomfortable with the satisfaction I'd felt playing laser tag in the eighties—shouting "Die, motherfucker!" at an opponent. That piece of me—the part that pretended not to like the brutal physicality of football or hockey, the part I masked with a love-everyone ethos when my instinct was to hit the asshole—

wanted just once to know what it was like to put my whole weight behind a punch.

I was in the thick of it on the dance floor, throwing my body against other bodies, gulping beer from the red cups Joey wisely doled out over pint glasses as three guitars shredded the sound system with a wall of electric noise and *rat-a-tat-tat* beat. The floor was slick and the chandelier lights swung as tables were hauled outside and people jammed into the space in front of the band. None of us cared what they were playing. Vaguely, I was aware of a crowd at the back of the bar, gaping.

After thirty minutes, I was out of breath and grinning from ear to ear. I'd thrown beer at one or two people, including DJ, who was clearly shocked and hurt, until he slammed right into me. *There, even.* I had shoved and been shoved. My hair hung in hanks against my neck, my skin as slick as the painted wood floor. My heart pounded.

"Oh. My. God," said Oody as I walked outside. The band was as loud outside as in; the front windows vibrated and shook. Oody wagged her head back and forth, grinning as if she'd just heard the most delicious piece of gossip, and I began to laugh. Loud and chortling at first, then deep. I couldn't stop.

The weight of a thousand bricks lifted from me. I grew lighter and lighter, euphoric.

"That was awesome," I shouted. Cameron, sporting a black motorcycle jacket and spiked hair, came by and slapped me on the back. "Good dancing, Karen," he said, and sloshed beer from a pitcher into my cup.

I took a gulp and looked at the bats swooping and twirling above. It was just past 8:30 P.M., not yet dark. My throat felt raw, my limbs like spaghetti.

"Okay, I'm done," I announced, and together, Oody and I walked arm in arm up the road to my truck.

On the hill across from the Merc, the mothership, a house with a giant peace sign on its face, lit up the darkening sky. The band played "I Wanna Be Your Dog," and Oody and I howled the words as loud as coyotes.

From the Merc porch, someone yelled, "Night, Karen."

Chapter 10

Fuck T. S. Eliot

In late October, I watched a bobcat hunt mice in the yard. If I hadn't caught its four-legged pounce out of the corner of my eye from where I sat near the window at my computer, I would have never seen it; its thick coat matched perfectly the tawny tint of dead grass on the berm where it lay. The animal took its time, surprising for so late in the morning, when the sun was clearly up and there weren't any shadows to skirt: Bobcats are notoriously shy.

I moved to get a better look at its muscular, bulldoggish body, its old-man face and tufted ears as Elvis lay oblivious beneath my desk, kicking his feet and uttering the muffled, heartbreaking cry a dog makes dreaming. He was clearly aging now. He didn't sense the world outside the cabin as he once had. In the last year, he'd developed a thyroid problem—"a classic geriatric disease," the vet said. Medication fixed his flagging energy levels and appetite, but his silky lanolin-scented coat had grown brittle and thinned in patches along his tail and the backs of his legs, revealing pink skin. He shivered on cold mornings.

There is an indignity to aging.

I'd seen it with my mother, who'd grown elderly. There was no other word for it. Just sixty-seven—she was too young not to be able to drive, too young to be so feeble. Too young for the way her memory shimmered like a mirage. *And yet.*

Blame it on her aneurysm, a beast that continued to be a problem. A scant three years after the Arizona trip, Mom had another procedure—with a new specialist in Denver—and then another. The coils continued to shift, surfing accumulated clots and blood. Three stents had been placed, one inside another, in an effort to stabilize the twenty-five-millimeter gap, but the aneurysm stubbornly took on more blood. It pulsed like a tiny beating heart at the center of my mother's brain and shoved itself against her spinal cord, causing weakness and dizziness. I sat with her through routine quarterly angiograms meant to track changes in size and the gaps between coils, and even those took their toll. Each time, my mother emerged with more memory depleted, more of her strength sapped. She had gone back to needing a walker and was on oxygen all the time. She endured grimly, as if watching a movie she didn't like, but I knew beneath her stoicism lay a well churning with disappointment, with fear.

Elvis, on the other hand, bore his failing physique with typical panache. I bought him a fleece jacket—powder blue with black inserts—and he looked even more handsome—sporty and athletic. He was still his goofy self—just slower and frankly, not as much of a pain in the ass. Gone were the days of long hikes. Instead, Elvis was happy to walk out to the peeper pond or down to the spring and back, and then spend the rest of the time watching the world from the deck or dreaming below my desk. *I* was the one who fretted. He was almost thirteen, officially geriatric. I thought about his mortality more and more.

Of course I'd nearly lost him when he was six. It was Valentine's Day and I had just returned home to Wisconsin and Elvis after a monthlong residency in Florida—my big push to kick-start my dissertation, a book of short stories. I listened to Garrison Keillor read love poems on *Prairie Home Companion* and composed a funny one for Elvis, who hadn't been eating, and sent it to the show. Earlier that day, I'd taken him to the vet because he was having trouble getting up the stairs, but the diagnosis was vague—and the vet had insisted on waiting for the Monday lab results before treating him. I'd insisted on taking Elvis home instead of having him held over the weekend. Hours later, Elvis, too weak to get up, began convulsing and I had to wake a neighbor who helped me carry him to my truck.

His disease, a form of anemia in which the body attacks its own cells, was diagnosed with a quick smear of blood on a slide. The clinician, who was young and short and had dark hair, called me into a room off the waiting area where there was an overstuffed couch and a box of tissues.

"It's a very bad disease," he said, "most dogs die."

"What do you mean?"

The treatment was expensive, a crapshoot because of timing and complications, he said. I might spend thousands and Elvis could still die.

"You might want to consider ending his suffering."

It was difficult enough to think of my dog as diminished, but the possibility of his dying was an idea I flat-out refused. He'd always had such life. To the doctor, the matter was one of investment, a bad bet. It was true: I had no money. But I would not put a price on Elvis' life. I felt an instinctual tug in my gut, a primal urge to protect my own. Elvis was still alive; there was still hope.

"Treat him," I said.

That night I got calls every two hours from the hospital.

During the first, the vet told me Elvis was so anemic he was "within points of dying." He needed a blood transfusion, the first of three, to "buy time" while the doctors waited for the immunosuppressant drugs to stop his body from attacking his blood cells, and then a bone-marrow tap, an ultrasound. With each call, the estimated cost climbed. And each time, I said, "Yes, go ahead."

I lay awake. It was too quiet in my apartment, the top half of a house in Milwaukee's Riverwest neighborhood. I watched the cloudy, city-lit sky from bed, astonished at the hole left by Elvis' absence—the familiar circle, thump, sigh of him settling in for the night. In the morning, there was no body following me around as I got dressed, no nuzzled request for a walk.

I drove to the clinic with Elvis' bed, his favorite toy, and one of my shirts. He lay on his side, moving only his tail up and down in a weak greeting. An IV dripped medication and fluids. His stomach and a patch on his hip were shaved.

I tied a picture of the two of us in Colorado to the bars of his kennel, a six-by-four space away from the other stacked kennels, and placed my shirt beneath his head. Elvis licked my fingers. As I lay down next to him and stroked the soft underside of his paw with my thumb, he relaxed perceptibly and fell into a deep rest.

That morning, I spoke with another vet on Elvis' case. She was in her thirties, with a wide-open face and short blond hair. She answered my questions, explaining that Elvis' diagnosis—immune mediated hemolytic anemia (IMHA)—was indeed a "bad disease," and no one knew why dogs got it. Patiently, she repeated the names of medicines and procedures as I took notes, sometimes crying as I did.

"What are his chances?" I asked her.

"About twenty percent," she said, as kindly as she could.

"What would you do?"

"Exactly what you are doing."

All night, I'd wrestled with questions: *Was I being selfish? Was my dog suffering? What was the best thing for him?* In that instant, I knew. I asked that the other vet be taken off Elvis' case.

"I want people who think he might live to treat him."

For five days, I visited Elvis three times a day, each time lying inside his cage with him for far longer than the twenty minutes I was allotted. The staff gave me a wide berth.

"He's better when you're here," one doctor observed.

Once he was released, his condition was guarded; Elvis still might die. His blood levels needed constant monitoring, first every two days, then twice a week. Slowly, his numbers climbed. *Slowly.* In the meantime, he took an immunosuppressant cocktail and saline injections four times a day. He required three times as many bathroom breaks, and each time had to be carried up and down the stairs. At his doctor's urging, I cooked protein-rich meats paired with rice and root vegetables and served cottage cheese snacks. At first Elvis would take food only from my fingers. I needed help.

Karen Z drove with her dog, Sandy, across three states to shove a wad of "Elvis Fund" cash into my hand, staying for ten days. Together with Erin and Rex, friends from her Milwaukee days, she took turns nursing my dog when I was teaching.

Just before Karen left, I screwed up the courage to ask his internist, a tiny smart woman named Mimi, if Elvis would live.

"Yep, I think he will," she said, as if confirming the weather.

Joyous, I bought a turkey and we celebrated Thanksgiving in March. The four of us sat on the floor of my flat and toasted Elvis with sparkling cider and ate turkey and cranberry. Elvis licked mashed potatoes from my fingers and nuzzled thigh meat out of my hand. The Wisconsin sky was unusually blue.

Just let me get him home to Colorado, I prayed. *Just give me one more year.*

Since then, we'd had seven.

I looked down at Elvis sleeping beneath my desk and then out to the berm. The bobcat had vanished. I went out to look for tracks but found nothing, no paw prints, no bent grass. There was no indication he'd been there. The same was not true of my dog; he'd left his mark indelibly. Together, we'd persisted. Back inside, I roused him for a walk. One day his presence would be replaced by the unbearable weight of absence, but not today.

"I don't know what I am going to do without him," I told my mother, who had settled in low-cost senior housing, a sweet little bank of yellow side-by-side condos in Niwot, when she was strong enough to live alone. I left Elvis with her three days a week on my way to teach.

"I know, sweetie," she said, watching Elvis walk to the bedroom and lie down. The companionship was good for them both.

Since my mother's stroke, our relationship had softened the way ice does, losing its hard edge reluctantly in early spring. My mother had never been demonstrative, never one to hug or say "I love you." Too often, I was unsure if she liked me. I was nothing like her. When she got sick, my lingering disappointment was held in check by my sense of duty. *It's what you do.* There were times when her care felt like a huge weight and I dreamed of it drowning me in a dark sea. Then I woke, gulping for air. Yet, despite this, *something* existed between us: We'd shared a body. I *had* taken her name. Sometimes, my mother turned to me, telling me the story of my birth: "When I saw that you were a girl, I cried." Tears of joy.

We forged a delicate alliance: She accepted my constant reminders to see doctors and eat better and exercise *and* I accepted her appreciation and thanks. Both of us avoided raising ghosts. At first my mother would simply say, "I know you are just trying to take care of me." Later, she would tell me, "I don't know what I'd do without you."

Over time, Mom had become more the woman she might have been had she not married my father or been saddled with kids so early or had to work so damn hard all her life for so little. She charmed her doctors and store clerks. The man who owned the take-out Chinese around the corner knew her by name and often offered to deliver her food to her rather than make her walk. She laughed when I teased her about the way she drank Diet Pepsi—two fingers at a time in a short glass, *like some tough guy*, I said—or her silly proclamations: "I don't like vegetables!"

"Oh, *Mother*," I'd say, in an exasperated tone that made her laugh. Her mouth would curl into a crooked smile and then she'd start to giggle. The giggle gave way to an explosive laugh. She couldn't stop.

"Oh, *you*," she'd say, "you do this every time," shuffling toward the bathroom.

But as I watched her grow weaker, there was a creeping terror that the day was coming when she would not be able to live alone. What then? The heaviness of her own parents' infirmity in the years before Nancy was born was a grief from which Mom had never recovered. Without the help of her siblings, she'd moved her stroke-addled mother and father from Arkansas to our house in Colorado Springs, where they resided for almost a year before moving into a nursing facility. Too much bitterness clouded my mother's memory. I saw how easy it would be for the same bitterness to cloud mine.

In November, when the ground was frozen over with newly

fallen snow, I called Mom for our regular check-in. She was stiff, she said, "not moving very well." It took me ten minutes to parse "stiff" into the fact that she'd fallen the night before and it had taken her an hour to get up from the floor. This morning, she confessed, she'd spent nearly two hours getting out of bed and dressed to make coffee.

"I think I pulled a muscle," she sighed, "my legs aren't working."

Why didn't she call?

"I didn't want to bother you so late."

Mom's balance had been an issue since her stroke, but she had been falling more. More than she'd told me. I raced down the mountain to the emergency room. My mother had broken her hip.

At the hospital, I was told the recovery—eight weeks in a wheelchair—was long. It would also be grueling. A geriatric specialist recommended Mom move permanently to assisted living. I ignored him and did not mention the matter to my mother. Instead Nancy flew out over the Thanksgiving holiday from Portland, where she'd moved with her soon-to-be husband, just in time for Mom's release, and we tag-teamed her immediate care, arranging follow-up visits with doctors and scheduling physical therapy and home health aides to help with showers and cleaning. The most difficult task by far was pleasing my mother, who issued orders covering the smallest of details. We were directed how to make the bed, how to do the laundry, how to dust and clean. I started calling her "The General."

"Here, put this away," she'd say, handing me a magazine I'd dropped on the table.

But Nancy, who stayed with Mom, took the brunt of it. Mom didn't care for Nancy's cooking and wanted take-out pizza and frozen dinners instead. And then Mom urged her to let Ava, her toddler, "cry it out," offering, according to my sister, "more advice than I've gotten in my whole life" while she was there.

At the end of the week, Nancy and I combined efforts to cook everyone's favorites for Thanksgiving: doughy Parker House rolls for Mom, dried apple and sausage stuffing with homemade cranberry sauce for me, and *fratuda dusa* for Nancy, made from almond-flavored Cream of Wheat thickened with eggs and then rolled in graham crackers and vanilla wafer crumbs and fried. The dish, from a recipe descended from my father's family, had always been made, perfectly, by my mother, who could never remember how she did it.

"Use cream—no whole milk," she'd say, when I attempted it myself. "I can't remember if it's yolks or whites or both."

Nancy's effort was delicious, but it set up in soft lumps instead of blocks.

"Maybe, just the yolks next time," said Mom.

Nancy and I thought we'd get a big kick out of putting on a meal together, but the joy we might have felt in the effort evaporated when Mom picked at her dinner, saying she wasn't that hungry. We were all exhausted. My mother went to bed early that night, putting her headphones on and disappearing into the world of Art Bell and his conspiracy theories, while my sister sat Ava down in front of a Disney film and furiously texted with her husband in Portland. I retreated to the cabin, Elvis in tow.

Ten weeks later, after my mother had finally traded her wheelchair for a walker, it was Elvis' turn. That morning, he'd lifted his
leg on our regular walk and sprayed blood onto a bank of snow.

My brain raced ahead diagnosing causes—kidney failure, cancer. *Was this it?*

Back at the cabin, I placed two calls: one to Elvis' vet and the
other to Judith. I simply could not face this diagnosis alone. The
clinic was over an hour away, but Judith said she'd finish her cleaning
job early and meet me there.

It was a sunny warmish February day, the kind that seemed to
offer a small reprieve from high-altitude winter. Longs Peak was
winter white and pockets of snow covered the mountain but the plains
were golden and brown. Elvis nosed the air outside the window of
the truck as we drove north along the prairie. *He seemed fine.*

At the clinic, he wedged himself between Judith and me on the
exam couch as his vet explained the diagnosis: tumors in the bladder.

Lauren was a small woman, a runner, who had an internist's
curiosity for the way my dog never presented any problem in a
textbook fashion. She'd overseen his eighteen-months-long recovery
from IMHA after we arrived back in Colorado and, in the nearly
seven years we'd seen her, amassed two full medical folders on his
conditions: allergies, skin rashes, hair loss, arthritis, degenerative disc
disease, a thyroid condition, and now this. Through it all, Lauren
remained upbeat, treating Elvis' odd symptoms as a terrific game of
Clue. When we'd first met at CSU, where she was head of internal
medicine, it had taken me a while to realize that the "kids" at home

were a pack of rescue dogs. When she left for private practice, Elvis and I followed.

The good news, she said, was the tumors were small and slow growing. They responded well to medication, something that would also treat Elvis' arthritis.

Lauren smiled and stroked Elvis' head, looking at me. She knew.

"This is not the thing that will kill him," she said, kissing him on the nose.

*   *   *

I've long thought February was the cruelest month—the month of short days and no light, when it was no longer possible to tart up the fact of winter with holiday lights and sparkly pumps. In a move that was part chutzpah, part desperation, I'd hosted the first Fuck T. S. Eliot dinner back in grad school at CU, when I'd proclaimed dramatically it would "bring light to the darkened world." Then, I cooked for three days, delivering five courses to a caravan of my most colorful writer friends for what I promised would be "an evening of cuisine and bombast."

Now February was upon me.

For nearly fifteen years, I'd spent all of January preparing, ripping through stacks of cookbooks and food magazines the way I'd once eaten waffles. *Zoop! Zoop!* I dreamed up food pairings with the intent to dazzle and compiled lists of spectacular courses. Next came the theme, followed by a menu. One year, it was Four Seasons, featuring a spring artichoke mousse and autumn duck confit ragout. Tomatoey *pappa al pomodoro* for summer and rolled and stuffed flank steak for winter. Each course came with a pairing of wine and music. Another year, a beaded and tie-dyed bunch from Jamestown sat on the floor of the horse barn in Left Hand Canyon and ate Moroccan lamb tagine and *b'stella* with their fingers while we played a murder mystery set in a sixties-era commune.

Over the years, Fucking T.S. had been my distraction, a playful finger raised at the armpit of the year and my always too-tight budget. It was a happy kiss-off, my own holiday.

But it had always been entirely of my own making.

This year, I was bone weary, tired of taking care. I hadn't looked at a single recipe. January had been spent in daily battle with a mound of ice outside the screen door. The gutter had a new leak, and the endless freezing and thawing of the season made for a constant drip onto the deck. If I didn't tend it daily, I wouldn't be able to open the door. I used a shovel, a cleaver, a rolling pin. I did not own an ice pick. Ice melt fell through the deck cracks. Once I came home from the Merc and had to hack away in the dark with a brick I'd scrounged from the yard, as Elvis barked and whined inside.

This year, I decided, T.S. would be different. I would buy champagne and make dough, and invite my regular group of friends— people who talked as well as they ate—to bring ingredients for pizzas. I set the date for Valentine's Day and requested pizzas that appealed to the sensual, to sexiness and passion, flirtation and desire.

The night turned out to be frigid, even by February standards. Snowflakes peppered the air, teasingly, flying sideways in a blow-over that arrived on a strong wind shooting off the Continental Divide. This type of "storm"—sometimes thick swirls of snow—tended to be all bark and no bite. Nothing stuck. Elvis trotted outside to greet guests wearing his fleece, already feeling better. Inside, my cabin was cozy with a fire and tea lights flickering on every open surface.

Judith and David arrived first, bringing appetizers—asparagus and lamb marinated in rosemary that I tossed on the grill. Judith wore a thin berry-colored angora scarf I'd knitted her for Christmas, David a soft lavender dress shirt.

Elvis woofed loudly at the door just as we settled into the living room. Before I could get up, Giulia, a friend of Elizabeth's from Rome, breezed in, followed by Clint and Jac. Giulia, already statuesque, was dressed in a silk sheath and leggings with tall Italian leather boots. She was an art historian at CU, where I'd landed a lecture position, and an actress, who'd dubbed Italian porn and had a brief speaking part as Gay Tourist #4 in *Under the Tuscan Sun*. She spoke a half dozen languages. Her fiancé, Pawel, was coming separately with his friend Sid, who would otherwise be alone on his birthday. Sid was nice, but one of those wonky engineer types who couldn't seem to talk about anything but preliminary observational tests and trajectories. He wore his California blond hair too long, well past his shoulders, in a kind of mop-like curtain.

I served the lamb and asparagus, and watched Clint, a quiet, shy man, lean into Jac, who'd attended some of the earliest T.S.

dinners, when she was a single twenty-something grader for the CU English Department before becoming a corporate trainer and married mother of four children. Clint whispered in her ear, his hand softly touching her hair. Jac seemed disinterested, her blue eyes tracking another conversation, but there was tenderness in her husband's touch. He bent toward her with the familiarity of two people who have been together a long time. There was a shared language, an unspoken intimacy. For just one moment, I was transfixed by what passed between them.

Once Pawel and Sid arrived, I filled champagne flutes and we raised our glasses. "Fuck T. S. Eliot," we shouted.

As couples slipped into the kitchen, pizzas emerged. We ate "Naked Pizza," made with garlic and four types of cheese, and another with wild mushrooms and mint, called "Earthly Delights" that Pawel said smelled "like victory." Last was "The Titian," Giulia's of course, with mushrooms and truffle oil, dabs of fried sage and goat cheese covered with translucent sheets of prosciutto when it came out of the oven.

We rotated seating with each new pizza, taking turns sitting on the couch and my one chair, or the floor, where I scattered pillows and a zafu. Gone was the formality of table seating with place settings and stemware. Instead, we licked pizza-laced fingers and talked and laughed. There was a kind of intimacy missing from previous years. Perhaps the difference was in me. There was no hurrying to clear dishes, no urgency to plate the next course, no stacked pots in the sink. I simply took it all in. It was the easiest party I'd ever thrown.

And the most enjoyable.

But not for Elvis. Now a cranky old man, he stood at the doorway to the bedroom and barked once, twice. He wanted me to come to bed; he wanted everyone to leave. After he wandered restlessly back and forth between the two rooms, I urged him onto his bed and shut the door. Loud sounds bothered him.

We sang "Happy Birthday" to Sid as I brought out a torte layered with ground chocolate cookies and ganache and something called rocky road cream—and Sid smiled, happy as a sheepdog, and blew out the red and yellow and blue string candles.

Giulia moaned with every forkful, licking her plate dramatically and saying something in Italian that she refused to translate.

"Sometimes," she said, "you need another language."

*   *   *

It had been my best T. S. Eliot party—in part because, for once, I'd simply let it unfold.

After everyone left, I washed the few dishes and glasses. The wind had finally stopped and the world was perfectly still. I could hear the deep whisper of Elvis' breathing from the bedroom. A waxing moon shimmered through the kitchen window, and aspens were silvery ghosts against a star-filled sky. An owl hooted across the snow-covered meadow. To some, it was a lonesome sound. In fact, *Aren't you lonely?* was the question most often asked of me after *Aren't you afraid?* My answer was taped to my computer, something

Natalie Goldberg had been told by the Zen master Katagiri Roshi: "Anything you do deeply is very lonely." When I first read the words, they were an anthem: I would embrace a solitary life and not be afraid. I wanted them to remind me of what I'd chosen, that space and solitude was the right thing for me.

There were indeed times when mountain living was lonely, but being lonely, the way Roshi meant it, I'd come to realize, was not really about isolation at all. Instead, it was about embrace: *Lonely* is a word that describes what it means to live profoundly. Moving deeply in the world, you let the thousand distractions fall away and you become more authentic, more who you really are.

Only on its surface, lonely was a reckoning—the price of sinking in—but it was not terrible. And as a result of so much time and space, seasons and land, I'd uncovered so much tenderness. It did not make me weak. And, paradoxically, I touched *more*. "Only after we have discovered [the world] for ourselves," writes Wendell Berry, do "we cease to be alone."

I looked out the window. It was a beautiful landscape. A lovely quiet night.

I blew out the candles and slipped into my bed, pulling a pillow to me, relieved and a bit sad to be on my own again.

Chapter 11

The Book of Mornings

J ust before his fourteenth birthday and five years after I'd moved to the cabin, Elvis was diagnosed with cancer. A lump on his back had tripled in size over the summer, and the biopsy exposed blood mixed with cells. A bad sign. The surgeon who removed the mass—a hemangiosarcoma—couldn't get the whole thing.

"To do that," he said, "I'd need to take half your dog."

The tumor was bellicose, I was told, the prognosis poor. Even if Elvis were to have chemo and far more costly radiation, it might buy him only a few months.

"How long?" I asked. *Three to nine months.*

Of course I wanted to stop time.

My first reaction was to thumb my nose at death. To make a spectacle in celebration of my dog. I would cast Elvis' paw print in bronze, I would make T-shirts with his picture on them, along with the words THE FAREWELL TOUR.

But I would prepare for it nevertheless.

Days later I celebrated Elvis' birthday on the day in November when I'd adopted him from the humane society, making roast chicken and mashed potatoes, a meal Elvis loved and one we'd shared on Sunday nights that first desolate year I lived in Wisconsin, when it was just the two of us in a house in a small port town. Although chicken had long since been replaced by duck and other allergy-friendly proteins on Elvis' menu, that night, I drank pinot noir and lovingly fed my dog slivers of thigh meat as he licked my fingers appreciatively. He wore a T-shirt tied in a knot to cover the eighteen-inch suture line inside a wide rectangle stretching between his shoulders and butt. Afterward, I gave him a few spoonfuls of vanilla ice cream and a birthday cookie I'd gotten at the pet store.

A few weeks later, Ryan, Judith's daughter, arrived to take pictures. I wanted at least one good photo of us together—but it was the dog who was photogenic, not me. The three of us walked out to the peeper pond. By then, Elvis felt frisky enough to pounce and play, galloping ahead as Ryan clicked away. Then, she posed us among aspens, near a rock outcropping, and crouching on the patchy winter ground. The sky was full and blue. Each shot revealed the dog I knew: Elvis flipping to roll in the snow, Elvis bowing and lunging to play, and Elvis flying, midleap, across a white embankment. In one he nuzzles my cheek; in another, I am holding him tight, my grin as wide as his own.

In the end, it wasn't anything I'd planned that stuck me to the days and made our time memorable. Instead it was something quite small. At the cabin, mornings had always been my ritual. I rose just before the sun, meditated, started a fire in the woodstove if it was cold, heated water and ground coffee beans for the French press.

By then, Elvis would be out in the yard, marking bushes, sniffing for what had transpired in the night. He toured the berm in the summer; in winter, he skirted the edge of the road, checking on Paul and Teresa's to the west, and then headed east, chasing rabbit or coyote tracks to the Stricklands' before crossing back to the cabin. When I heard the *thump-thump-thump* of him leaping up the stairs, I opened the door and let him in, and settled on the couch with my notebook and a cup of coffee so inky and rich it tasted like espresso.

Then I watched.

I gathered the morning in my notebook like someone pulling laundry from the line. Everything went in. Whatever was offered: In winter, it might be chickadees at the feeder and junco picking seed from the railing and ground. The sharp smell of looming snow when the wind changed direction and upsloped across the mountain, or the moldiness of grasses emerging at the first thaw, after months beneath ice. Once, it was a moose, a cow, who surprised me in the early pink light of a late-winter dawn, strolling down the drive and through the northern meadow. I watched her long-legged stride scuff the frozen patches of dirt and snow, grinning as she took her time, moving toward the peeper pond.

In summer, it was the determination of the robin whose urgent call was the pulley upon which the sun rose, followed by a twittering chorus of hundreds of birds. I could smell the loamy scent of dirt as the first hummingbird buzzed to the feeder, as I counted the shifting colors in the garden and listened to the wind gather across the meadow. The air was alive with bees and butterflies; chipmunks chased along the rocks, a grosbeak stopped for a drink and a dip at the watering hole rock. Sometimes there was gunfire, target practice on a warm summer day.

I found a home in the details: the winter wind, the first hint of sun, the color of dawn; the ticking sound the woodstove made when it was heating; the creak of pines, full of sap in summer, and aching, frozen in winter; the beauty of bare aspens against a winter sky, the quality of snow—soft, fat, sharp, stinging; the antics of animals, like the crow who sang *boop-Bee-do, boop-Bee-do* over and over from the top of a ponderosa on a summer day; clouds making pictures across the sky, or shrouding the Indian Peaks with weather—and that same sky, whose blue was the deep translucent blue of dreaming, whose moods reminded me that each day was its own imperative, the architect of it all.

Day after month after season, the practice of taking it all down became meditation and I, an observer of place. And then its guardian.

In the same way, I began collecting mornings with my dog. Weirdly, six months before his diagnosis, Elvis had begun nuzzling me awake. As soon as I stirred in the dim morning light, he stretched and padded to the side of the bed, inching his nose across the mattress in greeting, something he'd never done. "Good morning, handsome," I'd say, and stroke the fur fanning out from his cheeks and pull affectionately on his ears. He moved closer, placing a paw on the mattress. An invitation. Carefully, I'd help him up, hoisting him by his harness, and he'd settle along the length of my body. Together, we greeted the day.

In those first weeks after his diagnosis, I was in a panic. I wanted to do so many things. But in the stillness of one morning, I stopped, thinking suddenly of the way I'd gathered the days on the mountain. Here was another moment, another detail. To mark it, I raised a silent *thank you*. In this way, I collected each morning with neither the calendar watcher's sense of time running out nor the dread that the end might be near, but with genuine happiness that Elvis was with me *this one day*.

Miraculously, weeks passed into months into seasons. And my boy was still with me.

SPRING

Four feet of snow and the power out. I had been counting the catkins on the aspens in the front yard, a sure sign of an early spring, but an April storm leveled them. With Elvis in my truck, I drove haltingly to Jamestown, where, undeterred by weather, JAM was putting on a play, a farce written by seven people in town, and I had the part of Effie, a dim-witted housewife who cheats at a Scrabble game with another couple. The evening goes comically awry when the couple tries to teach her a lesson, tricking a fawningly patriotic Effie into believing her home had been invaded by terrorists.

Jamestown was a mess of cars and piles of snow. But DJ borrowed a couple of generators to run lights and heat, and the play went on to a packed town hall. People walked with flashlights and headlamps through streets crowded by three- and four-foot-high walls of snow. It seemed like two weeks before Christmas instead of two weeks until the beginning of May.

Snow fell hard for two hours as I sashayed across the stage in a polka-dot dress and pumps, raving about evildoers and George W. Bush. By then, the four-mile, fifteen-hundred-foot climb up Overland Road was a single track, cut by the plow heading back to Boulder. When it came time to head home, I shoved my truck into second gear, trying to keep my momentum up, but ground down to first as my progress slowed on the snow-packed switchbacks, and the mountain, the valley, even the edge of the road dissolved in a thick curtain of snow. Every single white-knuckle drive I'd ever had was trying to get home, long after the plows stopped, in the gut of a storm so bad I could see neither the sides of the road nor a scant ten feet in front of my truck. If you stop, you're stuck. If you drift too much, you could drive right off the edge of the road and barrel down an embankment. Worst of all: An oncoming car might plow right into you.

Twenty breathless minutes later, I arrived home, only to get the 4Runner stuck in the middle of my driveway. I left it and waded with Elvis through knee-deep snow to the cabin.

The landscape padded and hushed, I drifted off to sleep buried beneath piles of down, only to come crashing awake at the sound of cabin-shaking thumps, sheets of snow dropping in heavy piles from the overladen limbs of trees. Each time, Elvis gave a startled series of barks and then curled back up while I lay, wide-eyed, listening to wind scratch and rustle against the walls of the cabin.

When the thaw finally arrived, in mid-May, the peeper pond was as full as I'd ever seen it, flooding the trail Elvis and I skirted in search of pasque flowers and the first purple vetch. He'd long since recovered from surgery and seemed fine. He'd lived longer than three months. In celebration, we took our first spring hike with Judith and her Anatolian shepherd, Kafka, up the steep route to the Blue Jay Mine bordering Jamestown to the south. Elvis charged ahead, showing off, his breath coming in a series of exhaled and rhythmic *hah-hah!*s. His old-man pant. He seesawed back and forth as he climbed.

By the time we reached the top of the incline, I was breathing as hard as my dog. We paused in a tiny meadow, where a single yellow cactus bloomed, and gazed toward Porphyry, the mountain bordering the north side of Jamestown across the canyon.

Elvis stumbled. Twice.

"I think this was too much for him," I said to Judith as I watched him weave drunkenly. I grabbed his harness to steady him, but his pant was more than fatigue.

After ten minutes, he had not recovered. His front paws splayed out, as if he was standing on the deck of a rolling ship.

When we opted for the short way down, across the meadow toward Jamestown, I didn't notice the early green grasses poking up alongside melting patches of snow or the heat of the sun on my winter-worn skin. Instead I held Elvis' harness like he was a piece of luggage. He couldn't seem to get his back legs to work. His tongue hung like a limp piece of meat from his mouth. He rasped, then staggered as I led him toward a creek, his body listing from side to side. He bent and then fell.

I could not let go of my dog as Judith drove us down the mountain to the vet, where Lauren delivered the news: She was certain as she could be that Elvis had suffered a stroke.

"Something caused a bleed in his brain," she explained. "Generally these things resolve on their own, unless the cause is a tumor." And then, she said, it would get much worse. He could have a "major episode," a seizure. He could die. But he might also live. Only an expensive MRI would confirm what had happened, and it would not, Lauren said, change a thing.

We'd have to wait and see.

Uncertainty piled up in my mind like birds landing on a telephone wire. I didn't want to be alone. At home, Elvis was too nauseated and too unsteady to eat. I called Judith. An hour later, she showed up with two bottles of wine, some good dark chocolate, and Kathleen, a friend from our small book club, who'd brought her *True Blood* DVDs. Together, we sat on the couch as Elvis slept on my feet. Judith opened the wine.

"What are you going to do?" she asked, ever down-to-earth and forward looking.

"I don't know." I knew as well as she did that when the time came, I would likely have to decide *for* Elvis. "If this is it, I hope it's really clear."

"I think it's getting close," said Kathleen. I nodded, willing myself to think only of the glass of wine in my hand, the kindness of company.

SUMMER

Summer arrived, and my ticket paid for, I spent the solstice eating *lardo* and pizza Margherita in Rome before traveling to Umbria to perform Giulia and Pawel's wedding at a small *agriturismo*.

Before I left, I'd kissed my dog. "It's okay if you decide to go," I whispered. And I meant it.

"There is nothing more you can do," Lauren had said. "You've done the best you can. *Go.*" Her words were a kindness, a gentle reminder that Elvis and I'd had so many days together.

On a still cool morning, I took a picture of Elvis wearing his new white fisherman's sweater meant to cover his still patchy and tufted back as I hugged his dog sitter, an old friend, hello, and headed to the airport.

The Roman air was thick on my skin and smelled acrid and sweet. I had the traveler's sense that I could remake myself as I marveled at unfamiliar birds and blossoms, along with the Roman lifestyle, with its late-night dinners and laissez-faire arrival times. There is a kind of perspective in the new. For years after his IMHA, I'd wrung my hands about leaving Elvis, convinced my absence had a hand in getting him sick. For the first time, that all fell away. I *had* done my best.

I stayed with Elizabeth, my grad school pal, who had a pristine flat overlooking the tree-filled courtyard of a cloister. Her perfect Italian allowed me to buy lovely Barolo-cured sausage in the Campo de' Fiori and haggle for ridiculously cheap Vietri plates in Orvieto. In Fabro, I blessed Giulia and Pawel's union with poetry and celebrated the "love shared by two independent beings." The act was merely symbolic—they'd gotten legally hitched in May in their own backyard with Sid and me as witnesses. As they placed their hands over a loaf of bread Pawel's mother had carried all the way from Poland—a tradition called a *zrekowiny*—I covered their overlapping fingers with lace and invoked Neruda: "Two happy lovers make one bread."

Twelve days later, Elvis greeted me with his typical *whoo-whoo* and sniffed my hands, my face, my legs, even my neck and feet. It had been the longest we'd been apart in eight years. He'd lost some weight, but his energy was good and his balance restored. We entered the summer together, walking each day around the peeper pond to watch nesting ducks and swallows twirl in air. When he was strong, we walked as far as the fairy forest, in search of columbine.

I spent more days in the hammock, reading or watching clouds, Elvis lying nearby. I planted echinacea, more lavender, and black-eyed Susan in a new garden plot I carved out between the house and the shed, and tried not to wonder if Elvis would live to see its bloom.

In July, I hosted my father and his wife for dinner, serving the sausage I'd smuggled back in my suitcase. Since the fire, Dad and I had formed the wary, overly courteous connection of former adversaries, and it had been on his donated miles that I traveled to Rome. To celebrate, I served tomato salad with anchovies and pizza Margherita with arugula, followed by skirt steak. We drank Barolo out on the deck in the warm summer air. It was pleasant, *fun* even, but it was enough. He was the same man.

FALL

Fall arrived burning and gold as Elvis officially outlived his prognosis. The summer pushed headlong into autumn days, shoved by a late-season wildfire in Fourmile Canyon, just two ridges away. As I watched the curling wave of velvet orange and red flames from the overlook no more than a half mile from the cabin, I realized so many things were at an ebb. Elvis nosed the bushes, sniffing for chipmunks and rabbit while I traced the column of black smoke into the air. He didn't see what I saw.

The fire burned out of control for almost a week, claiming more than a hundred homes. Left Hand Canyon, just over the hill, had been evacuated. And Gold Hill, the next ridge beyond that, was on fire. The Jamestown fire chief said battling the fifty-foot flames was "like fighting fire in hell." Thick curtains of smoke draped the cabin in a fog. Finally, I packed my truck with a box of my journals, the pumice bear fetish, some photos of Elvis, and loaded my dog to spend the night at Giulia and Pawel's. My truck would remain packed for the duration of the burn. Whenever I left the mountain, my dog and my computer were in tow. The decision of what to take was easy, my priorities pared down.

The aspen changed overnight. I had been too busy watching the other fire and missed their slow light creeping up the mountain. As important as marking newly emerged flowers in spring, the ritual of watching leaves edge toward gold and red along the canyons draining toward the Front Range slowed down the leap from summer to winter. Fall always felt a bit frantic anyway—time slipped far too easily through the narrow neck of glass: There was wood to get in and stack, screens to be taken down, windows washed and pots cleared from the deck, hummingbird feeders removed and seed feeders hung from the ponderosa outside—but this year, the season careened.

The ebb of warm days was palpable. I lit my first fire of the season the first week of October—early. And although I spent each morning with Elvis breathing and saying my silent prayer of thanks, the days fanned like magazine pages.

WINTER

Twenty-five below and a long February night spent fretting the pipes would freeze or that Elvis would fail on this night, of all nights, when my truck was twenty miles down-canyon at the mechanic's. The icy rake of wind and frozen air was clearly too much for him. He looked frail for the first time, unstable on the ice outside, limping on frozen paws. His weight had plummeted to a shocking sixty-two pounds. There wasn't much muscle left on his back legs, his spine was an inverted V.

All the world was tenuous at these temperatures, when tree limbs snapped if you brushed past them and a layer of thick ice shagged every surface. It was so cold outside that the air froze in crystals that floated like the lightest snow. I rolled up a blanket and placed it in front of the door, where a patina of ice clung to the molding's bottom metal edge. The prayer shawls were pulled down, and I'd tacked another blanket over the biggest window in the living room. A space heater sat near the open cupboards, and all the faucets were on a drip. I worried about a power outage causing the heat lamp on the water pump to go out and then I'd have to chisel into the pump housing at the corner of the cabin, flanked by two feet of snow.

Elvis slept in his fleece as the temperature in my unheated bedroom plunged into the forties. I broke my no-evening-fire rule to keep a small oak-fed blaze going overnight, but I kept the heavy bedroom door firmly shut. Beneath a sleeping bag piled on top of my thick down comforter, I lay awake listening to Elvis' breathing.

The cold this winter had been a will breaker. Or perhaps I was simply tired of shouldering everything alone. My mother had been ill again. I'd had nearly two years and more than half a dozen emergency room visits, including the one for her broken hip. After another round of consultations and angiograms in Denver, Mom was scheduled for an experimental procedure in late May.

"I think we have to try," said Dr. Free, who'd done hundreds of successful simulations and would be performing the live technique with another doctor for the first time.

Nothing lasted forever, not even this cold, I thought. In the morning, I stoked the fire and sat on the couch with Elvis, who gave his full weight to me. I curled my hand around his cheek and held him, glad for one more day.

CODA

Just before the official advent of spring, Judith arrived as the sun sank behind the trees, the lengthening days perceptible. Plunking down a bottle of wine, she went immediately to my freezer, helping herself to a stash of chocolate I kept there. Elvis stirred in the bedroom and came out, greeting Judith in that happy husky way, while I poured the wine into deep glasses and carried them to the couch.

Judith had lost twenty pounds over the winter, after a terrible bout of walking pneumonia. She'd become so tiny, she wore her teenage daughter's clothes—leggings and jeans and short tight dresses, things Judith never wore. Her naturally chipper and let's-get-on-with-it self was tamped down—her eyes dulled, her inclined-to-grin face crumpled. She looked haggard.

She confessed she hadn't been sleeping. I asked about her mother, wondering if that was the cause.

"Good, for now," she said, shrugging.

Judith had twice flown home to England in the last six months to be with her ailing mum, but there was something else, something she said she "couldn't tell"—strange for us. Whatever it was, it had been going on for months and months.

"I'm starving," Judith announced.

I got up and lit a candle on the table and plugged in tiny white lights wrapping the wall tree. And then pulled out my new Vietri plates decorated with hedgehogs and bulls and poured a generous serving of polenta into each. On top of this, I spooned beef stewed with red wine, packed with mushrooms and peas.

"To spring—any day now," I said hopefully, raising a glass.

"Yes," said Judith, a little too brightly.

Her eyes closed as she swallowed a mouthful of stew.

"My god," she said. "I'd forgotten I liked food."

We drank more wine and talk turned to my mother.

"Hopefully, Steve will fly out for the procedure in May, I am registering at Tilt."

Judith nodded.

Finally, I said, "Okay, spill. *What is going on?*"

Turns out David, who'd just celebrated his sixtieth birthday, had met someone. They had been emailing after a brief encounter at a coffeehouse in Mexico, the solo trip David took to celebrate his birthday in November.

"He thinks he loves her," said Judith.

Except for the pain on her face, my first reaction was to laugh out loud.

"How is that possible?" I said. According to Judith, they'd met at a cantina, talked for an hour or so, and then she flew home to Florida. They had been exchanging emails ever since.

I was certain of nothing except that I'd stepped into unfamiliar terrain. I had no idea what passed between people who'd been together for years, but my instinct was to take my friend's side, to villainize David. *Their marriage seemed so perfect.*

"What will you do?"

She shook her head. "I told him to go see her and decide."

I nodded. David had left five days ago. "Shit."

"She's twenty-eight," she said quietly. Half Judith's age. She pressed her fists to her eyes, sobbing, and Elvis got up to nose and kiss her cheeks. I pulled him gently back, petting him with one hand while I held Judith's with the other.

Then, just as quickly, she pulled herself together again. That stiff upper lip.

"And now?"

"I wait." She shrugged.

We sat, listening to the last of the fire in the stove. I leaned over to kiss her on the cheek.

"Motherfucker," I said.

She smiled. "Yeah, motherfucker."

After Judith left, I curled up with Elvis and thought how earlier we had turned back on our walk out to the peeper pond because it was too cold. Even his fleece hadn't helped. He snored softly as I stroked the sparse and scruffy fur along his back.

Elvis' gums had been inexplicably bleeding for more than a week. I often woke at night to hear him licking and licking. In the morning there would be a pink stain on his bed. I would have to take him in to see Lauren. Snow fell in thick clumps outside. The world felt tenuous. I held my breath. Really there was no guarantee what was to come.

PART IV

A Season of Voluptuousness

Chapter 12

Loving Elvis

The morning was clear and bright, almost unseasonably warm. A bit of wind shook the trees outside as I held Elvis' blue fleece beneath my cheek and chin. Sleep, if it came, had a raw edge. In the night, I'd heard an owl calling across the meadow, my window open for the sound of its wings.

Take care of my boy, I thought.

Giulia shifted on the couch in the living room and rubbed her face sleepily as I started coffee in the kitchen. She had stayed the night so I wouldn't be alone.

"Did you sleep?" she asked.

The house was so quiet. Empty.

I'd had seventeen months to prepare for the feel of this morning, the sense that there was too much space inside my tiny cabin. And still, it slammed into me. Where was the animal who had tracked my movements for almost fifteen years?

The ending began two days before, after a midnight visit to the emergency clinic, quickly followed by an appointment with Lauren.

Lauren hugged me at the door of the clinic and bent down to kiss Elvis' nose.

"Hello, handsome," she said.

An ultrasound showed new tumors piercing the bladder wall and allowing fluid to leak into Elvis' abdomen, causing some amount of pain. In a few days, his organs would start to fail.

"From there," Lauren said, "things will go very fast." She could send him home with a fentanyl patch, but we would have only two days to say goodbye.

I'd been worrying about losing Elvis almost from the day I got him. Now the end had arrived and the shift was seismic. It wasn't death, whose footsteps I'd long been hearing like an echo in a canyon, that I feared, but the complete reconfiguring of my days and myself.

"I don't know who I am," I said to Lauren as I hugged her goodbye, "without my dog."

*   *   *

In Jamestown, Elvis was a bit of a celebrity. People saw his white head poking from my 4Runner window whenever I worked at the Merc. After he'd had his back tumor removed, Joey had let me bring him inside while I cooked and waited tables, and Elvis would curl up near the kitchen, rising, tail wagging a friendly hello whenever someone walked inside. He loved people. Once, I found him stopping a line of cars outside the Merc, jumping up to give each driver a kiss. Together, we had marched with Joey's kazoo band on more than one July Fourth and then had our picture taken with the rest of the town standing in front of the Merc or down in the lower park by a fire engine.

"Where's Elvis?" people frequently asked. He was the twin of my days. My answering machine announced the "home of Karen and Elvis." My mother sent him birthday cards. Friends knew when they invited me to their houses, Elvis would be in tow.

I'd always said the dog was the nicest thing about me. Elvis loved others naturally, in a way I never could. He was my ambassador of goodwill, my heart, and now I'd have to let all of that go.

Just a week earlier, I'd watched in the light of early morning as Elvis hunted tracks in the yard, sniffing for coyote and fox. He ambled awkwardly between rocks, skidding sideways on slick surfaces, his mind riding herd over a body that slipped where it should step, stumbled where it should bound. He had no idea that he was old. His gait was stiff and stilted; his paws didn't pad so much as stab the ground. But while his body with its warts and bald patches and wasting muscles was verging on frail, his mind—that curious, happy husky brain—was all there. He cantered off to investigate the morning. When he returned, bounding through pine trees and still-bare aspen, he was propelled by sheer enthusiasm, as if he'd discovered the most wonderful thing. Hoarse and breathless, breathing his smoker's wheezing *hah*, Elvis' grin said it all—*it was a great day outside*. I let him inside, but he was all excitement, as if to say, "Hey, it's spring—let's get out there!" He pawed me where I sat on the couch writing, and gave me that you-know-what-I-want look, then went back to the door.

Exasperated, I let him out again, this time fleeceless, to explore the thawing yard, the new spring birds, more tracks in the mud near the woodpile. He went back and forth, in and out, until finally I gave up, and together, we walked to the Cushman Ranch, circling the lake at the center of the sloping grassland, the edges lined with pine and fir, a two-track dirt road ambling through. It was my favorite vista on the mountain. There was an old barn and ranch house on one ridge. In the summer, cows waded through bluestem and switch-grass for a drink of water. Elvis trotted out ahead of me, loping around the far edge of the lake, a white spot on the horizon. The air smelled of earth and mold. I wore a jean skirt and a fleece jacket and my battered white cowboy hat. Spring was upon the mountain.

That day, he begged for a walk—that was the dog I'd always known—but a week later, weakness and vomiting sent us to the ER. That was it. There was no slow decline, no agonizing months-long end where I had to question over and over, *Is it time?* I simply knew.

And I had a plan.

I picked Saturday, two days after our visit with Lauren, giving me one last full day with my dog. Lisa, Elvis' acupuncturist and a vet, lived right across Overland Road and offered home euthanasia. I called my friends, giving each a part in Elvis' send-off.

But Elvis spent an uncomfortable night after our visit with Lauren. His breathing was labored and he couldn't settle. I slept at his end of the bed, my hand on his back and chest. In the morning, he was so stoned from the opiate that I had to carry him down the steps to the yard, where he wobbled, then squatted to pee just two steps from where I placed him, his gaze unfixed, distant.

I could tell it wasn't the pain but the medication. Confused and anxious, Elvis fought his morphine haze. Before I could help him climb back into the house, he attempted the stairs and fell backward, landing with a deep grunt.

"Hold on, sweetie," I said, picking him up like a calf and carrying him up the steps.

Inside, I removed the patch. Fading into a fentanyl fog wasn't the kind of end I wanted for my dog. Our days together had been carved out of Elvis' energy and sheer joy. His death would be too.

My first call was to Lisa. *Could she come today instead?* The next was to my friends, who shifted schedules and canceled classes and clients.

When I hung up the phone, I walked to the center of the cabin. My life had been grounded in a thousand tiny rituals—the lighting of candles, the eating of food, meditation, the making of prayers on paper I burned in the stove or in the prayer flags that hung outside my cabin. I'd welcomed seasons and asked for change. I had celebrated unions and births and survival. And now for the first time, I would celebrate death.

I didn't have a clear notion of what would happen to Elvis' spirit after he died, but I understood, it was my duty to make certain requests on his behalf. I have always felt that part of giving Elvis a proper life lay in giving him a proper death. I let my voice fill the cabin.

"Today is the day," I said, "let it be good."

In that moment, there was no power that would refuse me.

Then I walked into the bedroom and lay next to Elvis. He kissed me weakly and I began to cry.

"It's time, buddy," I explained. "Your body can't do it anymore." I rubbed his ears and ran my hands down his back. "I'll be right here with you."

Words spilled out. He was my best friend, my boy, I said. He would always be with me. Elvis looked at me calmly and continued licking me. I curled up next to him, listening to him breathe, my hand on his chest near his heart. We lay together for a long time just like that.

After a while, I got up and began moving furniture to make a space in the living room for everyone to sit on the floor with Elvis. Kathleen arrived first, nearly two hours early. A relief. I didn't know her very well, but I knew she loved dogs. Her quiet presence focused me; I calmly did what needed to be done while she sat quietly with Elvis.

I put soft music on and then made roast chicken and mashed potatoes for Elvis. By now I had given up trying to hide my weeping.

One by one, my friends arrived. Judith brought bells, Rainbow a book of poems. Jody, my friend of thirty years, brought Michigan juniper for a blessing before his send-off.

Unexpectedly, Karen Z arrived. We'd had a pretty big falling-out a few years back after I was one of three people working on the addition she was putting on her tiny cabin on Ward Street. Task completion was not Karen's strong suit, and too often, she made the process much harder for her niece, Rachel, and for me. Both of us had given up a month of summer and volunteered to help Karen—who was on a bare-bones budget, racing against a refinancing clock—and save her money. We poured foundation, painted the new walls, and tiled the house on a strict deadline. One day, after Karen's meddling ground our progress to a halt, I snapped and had what can only be described as a temper tantrum. Karen kicked me out.

We'd tentatively mended the most ragged parts of our hurt feelings, but we no longer walked dogs together or went out for a beer. Still, I'd mentioned to her at the Merc a few weeks ago that she might want to come see Elvis sometime soon. Karen had always been his champion. It occurred to me as she drove up that, *yes, of course,* she should be here.

Elvis tottered into the living room to greet Karen and settled onto his bed, as everyone took their place on the floor around him. I tried to get him to take some chicken and mashed potatoes from my fingers one last time. He sniffed and turned his nose away. The fentanyl had worn off—he wasn't groggy and muddled—but his attention was focused on the edges of the room. His eyes were dark, his gaze distant.

As we waited for Lisa, Judith sang "You Are My Sunshine," something I'd sung hundreds of times to Elvis while we drove down the highway together. In turn, each person told a story about Elvis. Rainbow apologized for not having chosen a poem ahead of time.

"But I opened this book just now," she said, "to this poem by Frank Yerby. I think it's perfect." The poem was titled "You Are a Part of Me." In it, the speaker, addressing the beloved, says he cannot regret their separation, "Knowing no magic ever can set free / That part of you that is a part of me."

We would forever be joined, this dog and I.

Lisa arrived and shaved a small spot for Elvis' injection. She gave him a bit of Valium to keep him calm and waited for it to take effect.

After a few minutes, Elvis looked at Lisa and then to the spot on his leg and directly back to her.

"He's ready," I said.

Holding his head in my arms, I looked him in the eyes and whispered, "You're my boy" and "I love you the most." I kept whispering into his ear and stroking him, my face pressed against his. His head leaned into me, in that affectionate husky way, and then, gradually, he gave its weight over to me as his heart slowed and the beats lightened.

"It's okay, it's all okay, you can go now."

When his chest was silent beneath my hand, Lisa checked his pulse as I whispered, "Good night, sweet prince." I kissed his nose and face: "You have my heart." Lisa nodded at me. Tiny bells tinkled inside the cabin.

After just a few moments, I sat up, my hand still on Elvis' chest.

"We have to go." My urgency was driven by the fact that I wanted Elvis cremated that day. I couldn't bear the thought of his body unattended, alone overnight. Karen Z had contacted a private pet crematorium outside Fort Collins, where I'd gone with her when Sophia died, and they'd agreed to wait for us until 4:30.

I had already put the backseat of the 4Runner down so I could ride with Elvis; his camp blanket—a red, white, and blue quilt left over from a Jamestown Fourth of July—was spread out in the rear of the truck. I picked him up as I had so many times, scooping my arms around his chest and butt, and carried him outside. Inside the truck, I lay next to him, feeling for the silky feathers of his paws and the velvet of his ears. Already his skin had stiffened, his muzzle no longer pliant and soft. I closed my eyes. Judith drove with Giulia in the front seat, and Karen Z followed with Sandy in her own truck. I ran my hands over the length of Elvis' body as the familiarity of him receded. By the time we reached our destination, an hour later, I knew his body was just that—a body. I kissed him one last time and removed his harness.

Lucille, a mirthful woman with red hair who lacked—*thankfully,* I thought—the syrupy deference of too many funeral home employees, greeted us as we drove up. She helped me take a print of Elvis' paw and handed me scissors to cut some of his hair as Karen Z smoked his body with Jody's juniper for blessing. Inside, Lucille and another woman loaded Elvis' body into a metal tray. Then she gave me a thick leather coat and gloves and told me to "push hard and quick—it will be hot."

This piece of Elvis' death was the most important. I pulled on the coat and gloves and whispered to Elvis one last time: *"Run!"* I said, and then I put my hands on his butt and shoulders as the oven door opened and the tray tipped, and shoved as hard as I could. We need a word for the stewardship of death. *Midwifing* will not do. The act is a ritual of returning, of giving back. And it is sacred.

Elvis' white fur went black the instant his body hit the heat. I closed my eyes, sobbing.

Karen Z and I walked along the Cache la Poudre while Giulia and Judith went in search of food. Cottonwoods lined the small creek. The sun warmed the earth beneath our feet.

After an hour, Lucille called us back. When she lifted the heavy metal oven door, only tiny pieces of bones remained. Lucille scraped the ashes and bits of bone with a long trowel into what looked like an assayer's tray. Shards that had once formed the skeleton of my dog's body glowed red, like coals. When they were cooled, Lucille picked through pink- and green-tinged fragments with long tweezers. I was reminded of the worry with which I'd picked through the ashes of my house, searching for things, fragments that would remind me of my life—all that I lost, who I was. This was different. I felt wonder, not desperation. Elvis' bones, his foundation, lay before me. I imagined the bones connecting and holding skin, I imagined them bounding and leaping. Each piece was precious, each an affirmation of the life we'd shared.

"These are minerals," Lucille explained, pointing to the colors on the bones. "He was a well-cared-for dog." She handed me the tweezers and let me pick out whatever pieces I wanted: a couple of toe bones, a slice of rib, part of the spinal cord, a tibia, and most amazingly two canine teeth.

"You are lucky," she said. "We rarely get those." The rest of the bones went into the grinder until what remained of Elvis was a fine ash—just enough to fill a plastic sleeve inserted, most ridiculously, into a recipe box decorated with blue flowers.

*   *   *

The next morning, Karen Z arrived just as I was pouring coffee. After Sophia died years before, when Elvis and I lived in Jamestown, she'd made me promise to bring Elvis up the street to go for our regular morning walk.

"If I don't do it, I never will again."

She was returning the favor.

Together with Giulia, we walked around the peeper pond, where just a few days before Elvis and I had been turned back by an icy wind.

The morning was bright and cool, not cold, the sky that Colorado blue that makes you think anything is possible. I wore my thinnest fleece. At the apex of the circle around the pond, in the place where you can turn and look back over the aspen-rimmed wetlands to Sawtooth and the rough edge of the divide, a single pasque flower grew, the first of the season. The season of renewal would follow close upon.

We walked without talking, watching Maggie, Karen's newest rescue golden, spin on the trail.

"She's happy," Karen said.

That night, I went to the Merc to listen to the Saturday night band and have a beer. Unusual for me. I wasn't sure if it was the emptiness of the cabin or the need to be with others that propelled me. I'd already gotten almost fifty emails from friends sending condolences about Elvis, and the QT message board lit up with tributes to my dog as word spread around town. Inside the dimly lit café with its pine-green floor and kitschy cloth-covered dome lights, nearly every person sidled up to me to tell me how sorry they were about my dog.

"I can't imagine you without him," said Miles, a man who wore a perpetual wide-eyed look of surprise, as if living was an act of astonishment and perplexity.

When I got home, I lay awake listening to the first thunder of spring rumble across the mountain, the echo coming from a distance, the mountain singing a song of change.

*   *   *

I knew Elvis had had a great life, that he was a lucky dog. But I was lucky too. The love of a dog is no small thing. Every moment of my days with him conspired to alter the architecture of my heart. My life was bigger, richer, deeper, and more profound because I'd taken the dog with the spiked collar home with me. He was my guru, my god, my bodhisattva.

Grief swept over me in strange waves. At first I wept openly—in front of strangers, on the phone to my grandmother, a pet lover, and to friends or walking alone, feeling as if grief was washing me clean. I did not feel broken. Instead, my sorrow was confirmation that I'd loved deeply. Elvis had needed me to hold the lamp up between the world of the living and the dead: This I did and was not undone. This was the work of love.

I thought I would sail through. *Hadn't I prepared?*

But grief carries a hundred faces.

In the days following Elvis' death I felt immense relief, a strange buoyancy. I was euphoric, my constant worry dissolved into lightness. Part of it was that I had, as Judith had said, "done good by Elvis." His passing was perfect: He lived until the day he died.

But after a week, when the shock wore off, a hollow, hungry feeling replaced my euphoria. I was certain I'd sense his presence in the days after his death. But I felt nothing. Instead, I moved through my routine as if he was still there—automatically rolling down the back window so he could stick his head out when I started the truck, waiting for the *thump thump* of his paws on the deck while I drank my morning coffee, listening for his breathing in the night.

Vexed, I called an animal communicator, a woman named Rhianna. I'd consulted with her a few times with good results: *He's not dying. No, he's not ready to go yet.* Through Elvis' illnesses and ailments, she'd been right every single time. I trusted her.

At first, I apologized, but she assured me that people frequently called after pets died. Sheepishly, I explained I was pulled in opposite directions: I knew Elvis was gone and yet, I was hollowed out by the feeling that I could no longer locate him in time and space. I couldn't feel him.

"I thought I would," I said.

Rhianna told me Elvis had "chosen to stick around" for a few weeks or months, "and then he's going to leave with the Spirit Pack." Listening, I imagined a collection of wolves sitting in a misty landscape in some ridiculous blue-and-silver-hued new age painting. The kind that was gauzy and sentimental and trite.

No, I thought. *Too ridiculous, even for me.*

She ended by telling me that "the guardian will come get him."

I hung up the phone, miserable. Death was death. The absence it left drained the color from my days.

The next day, I had my first panic attack. I came home from yoga after another tense drive up the canyon. Thunder rolled down the mountain as a curtain of fat wind-driven flakes assaulted the air. I couldn't see five feet in front of my truck. I arrived at a dark cabin with no dog to greet me and slipped into bed, my heart pounding, relentless. Then, I lay awake for four hours. My shoulders burned and my mind clicked on a heavy metronome in time with my heart: Too much yoga? Heart attack? I took Rescue Remedy and an aspirin just in case it was the latter and tried to breathe slowly and deeply as snow fell in roof-thumping *whomps!* from trees above.

The following day, the snow gave way to a warm spring wind and the landscape dissolved into puddles and ponds. The first bluebird appeared at the peeper pond, followed by mourning doves.

The following week more snow fell. I worried about the hummingbirds, who would return any day now. I hung up my feeders and tried to keep them clear of ice.

A few days later, it happened again. This time, I woke up terrified, my heart leaping like a spooked horse as a gust of wind slammed into the cabin. Shivering uncontrollably, I pulled my sleeping bag over my thick down comforter. I drank a bottle of water and again took aspirin and Rescue Remedy, trying to calm myself as the hours ticked on the clock and more wind howled outside. But my heart beat harder and harder, trying to sound the depths of the universe for Elvis. The next morning, I felt as if I hadn't slept at all.

By the third time it happened, the bears had emerged—I'd seen the first one at the intersection of Left Hand and James Canyon, but still no hummingbirds. This time, I picked up the phone. Judith, who had been prescribed way too many painkillers for a herniated disc following a car accident, had flown the coop for Boulder after an opioid-induced fight with the just-returned-from-Florida David that blasted the remnants of their marriage to bits; she could not come to the rescue. I called Jan, a woman from my mountain writing class who was an EMT on the Jamestown VFD, and left three SOSs without response. I tried Rainbow. It was 12:30 in the morning.

"I'll come get you," she said simply.

At her tiny log cabin on the banks of Jim Creek, she wrapped me in a blanket and made me Tension Tamer tea and put me to bed in the alcove where her son, Kofi, normally slept, while the rest of her family—her husband, son, and new baby, Juna—piled onto two queen-size mattresses shoved together on the floor of her bedroom, a framed-in, east-facing porch.

The next day, my heart burned again and my chest felt heavy. I went home to my empty cabin. Here was the underbelly of grief: I understood quite suddenly I'd been waiting for Elvis to return—as if, inexplicably, he'd been on a trip.

"He's not coming back, is he?" I said to my mother on the phone.

I missed his body, his presence. I wanted to *see* him.

I would carry that ache with me for a while. It would take me on a road trip to Taos and through a summer hiking alone on the mountain. I had to find a new way to love Elvis, different from the way I'd been loving him for almost fifteen years.

*   *   *

Seven weeks after Elvis died, I had a dream: I was at Judith and David's house, which was empty. Elvis had been left outside. It was night. Worried he'd be prey for a mountain lion in his aged and weakened state, I opened the door and called his name. Outside, a bunch of dogs gathered. They were all shapes and sizes, a collection of pound dogs, I thought. One dog got up when I called and came inside: It was Sandy, Karen Z's golden who had died over a year ago. I whistled for Elvis again and he appeared suddenly, as he often did on the trail, bounding out of nowhere and into the house, grinning. He had wings on his shoulders. Outside, a man who looked like an accountant with thick glasses, a short-sleeved dress shirt, and tie waved his arms. Elvis took one look at me and then at the dogs. Then he leapt up and flew through the ceiling-to-floor glass and disappeared.

In the Tibetan Buddhist tradition, the soul is said to wander for forty-eight days after the body dies. Its job is not to get lost, so that on the forty-ninth day it can reincarnate. I once saw a documentary in which priests kept vigil over the decaying body of another priest for seven weeks, singing prayers to help usher the soul into the next world.

That day marked the forty-ninth since Elvis had died. He'd been with me all along.

But I hadn't seen it: not in the raven who landed to eat Elvis' last meal—the leftover chicken placed on the stump outside—who held my gaze with its black mysterious eye for a full minute from the railing of the deck; not in an Elvis Presley song playing on the radio as I shopped for groceries or the owl I heard for three nights at precisely the same time after Elvis died; not in the feeling I'd had waking one night to a paw stepping on the bed. I wrote all of these things down in my journal, collecting pieces of the days without Elvis, too focused on seeing his body instead of his presence.

On the fiftieth day after Elvis' passing, I woke up laughing and crying. He had always undercut my prickly ego, my fuck-you attitude, my need to control every little thing. For every single time I'd wailed over the prospect of losing him, fretted when he wouldn't eat, shouted and cajoled for him to come back on the trail, and worried senselessly and sleeplessly about his health, his response had remained the same. It was encapsulated in the moment he did flip-flops in the snow as my house burned:

What a great thing it is to be alive.

Don't take any of this, least of all yourself, too seriously.

The only force strong enough to teach you this is love. Not the love of soul mates and candy hearts but the force that orders the stars, the heartbeat of the universe.

I'd learned from a very young age to isolate myself from people and from a world that offered up far too many dangerous uncertainties. I thought I was being smart. I would saddle up and ride off into the sunset, alone, armored up and invincible. But then Elvis inserted himself between my breastplate and skin.

I thought I was getting a companion to my days, a trail buddy, a friend, but in the end, Elvis stood at the threshold of the wild world, *the real world,* his tail fanning back and forth as he led the way. *Come on,* he said, *there's more between heaven and earth . . .*

And there was.

Chapter 13

Yajna: Fire Ceremony

In the blue light of an early August morning, I sat cross-legged, wrapped in wool blankets, before a fire rising from a deep ceremonial pit. It was 5:30. Around me: walls painted with images of Ganesh, the elephant deity, the remover of obstacles, and Hanuman, Rama's devoted monkey warrior, who leapt across an ocean with a mountain on his back. Outside, the forest air was tinged with the first damp earth smell of fall. Even though the mountain was still covered with summer-green grasses and leaves, there was an edge of decay, the mustiness of leaves beginning to brown. *All of it will be gone in a month*, I thought.

Across the tiered edges of the square pit, a twenty-something man with long curly brown hair and clear blue eyes chanted in Sanskrit, a language steeped in sounds said to reconfigure molecular structures. He drew pinches of masala from a bowl with his right hand, to his heart, before tossing the mixture of flax and rice into the flames. I did the same. Below us, pine logs bristled with sparks as smoke rose.

"The fire is sacred," the man had said. "It burns away karma. It purifies the soul."

"Swa-ha," I said, scattering masala to the rhythm of the pundit's prayer. *Let it be so.*

When I'd sighted the ashram from the long barrel of late spring, my life had been cluttered with work and worry and grief. I had anticipated a mountain summer of learning to be alone again, but all that had collapsed in the face of another emergency: My mother's delicate health, slipping these past years the way thimble-sized bits of snow calve along a hillside, was in free fall. My family would convene once again and resurrect the worst parts of ourselves. Instead of grieving, I'd spent the warming months of spring into summer engaged in chest-pounding displays with my brothers and sister over who would do what and when.

By then I was exhausted. Little is said about the ambivalence of caregiving. The burden of so much worry, so much responsibility, and the weariness and umbrage that develop over time. My brothers and sister invoked their families and their commitments as reasons for their limited engagement—all of it, legitimate— but because I was in such close proximity and because I had no family of my own, I could claim no such privilege. I felt a duty to my mother, but after six solid years of being her first responder, I needed *retreat.*

Shoshoni was the sister ashram to the great adobe and wood-domed building in Eldorado Springs just south of Boulder where Giulia and I attended yoga class on Monday nights. It was an easy choice—just thirty miles south of my cabin along the Peak to Peak Highway. I could escape for a week without the added burden of airplanes or a long drive or being out of touch in case my mother's condition suddenly deteriorated.

That morning, I was the only guest at the *Yajna*, the first daily ritual—before chanting, before yoga, before breakfast—at the ashram. Fitting to begin the day by burning the past—a reminder that all we have is the present. The temple was large enough to seat a hundred people, but it was just me and the pundit in front of the concentric red, white, and black squares that marked the fire pit. Outside, the day blossomed as the sun came over the mountain and light crept in. A mourning dove called, that aching *perch-coo* I loved, so full of longing. Smoke rose. *Swaha, swaha,* I chanted.

So much had happened.

*　　*　　*

In early May, three weeks before my mother's next aneurysm surgery, I'd gone to Taos with Giulia. Something tugged me south to the same place where I'd tried to escape the grief of turning forty and losing almost twenty years of work. Now, seven years later, it was the emptiness of my cabin, the absence of Elvis, a spring that continued to dump late-winter snow. It would be, I joked, the final leg of Elvis' farewell tour. Instead of the dog, I'd be taking his blue box of ashes.

An icy drizzle spit wet flakes on still-bare aspen in the yard. They landed with a slap, before melting instantly or puddling in clumps on the newly emerged lady's mantle. I wept as I carried my duffel bag and my yoga mat to the truck. By now, Elvis would have been seated in front, stubbornly insisting that wherever I went, he would too.

I put the bird seed pail inside the cabin door, hoping a hungry bear wouldn't nose its presence, and carried the trash, whose stink he surely would, to the truck for a dropoff at the Merc's dumpster. Last, I loaded Elvis' ashes.

"Come on, handsome," I said.

At the Merc, I gave a couple of dollars to Rainbow for the trash disposal and held her toddler, Juna, while Rainbow made a plate of hard-cooked eggs and crispy bacon for *El Patrón*, his morning ritual.

"Doggie," said Juna, smiling up at me.

"What?"

"Doggie!"

I looked around. No dogs on the Merc porch.

"Her new word?" I asked Rainbow, when she pulled Juna onto her hip.

She shook her head. "She's never said that before."

In Boulder, the weather was pure drizzle. I parked my truck in front of Giulia and Pawel's house. Like me, Giulia wanted a holiday. In the year since they'd been married, she and Pawel had been trying to conceive a child, but her forty-something eggs hadn't cooperated and the newlyweds were on the edge of IVF. Giulia burned for motherhood: Her urgency was the sharp bloom of a flare on a dark night. I, on the other hand, understood I was past all that now. When I was younger, I thought I'd have kids of my own, but

I kept waiting for *something*: a stable income, a partner, the feeling
I was settled. In the end, it was probably the circumstances of my
own childhood that provided the real roadblock: Secretly, I feared
I was doomed to repeat history.

And yet, mothering was my MO. I could see it in my relationships with friends, with Elvis, with my own mother. I'd been taught
to anticipate the needs of others, to go out of my way to fix things,
even at my own expense.

Giulia greeted me at the door with a Roman kiss (both cheeks).
She wore flared yoga pants, flat leather boots, and a purple scarf
engorged with flowers swirled with gold around her long, statuesque
neck. When serious, Giulia had the beatific mien of a Renaissance
saint, when not, the rubber-jaw goofiness of Harpo Marx. Behind
her, Pawel, who was pure teddy bear, greeted me with a hug and a
paper bag of croissants and lattes to go.

"E!" Giulia exclaimed, as I fitted Elvis' box behind the stick
shift of her Honda hybrid. Everyone had a nickname for the dog:
Karen Z called him *El* and *Handsome*, Judith and Rainbow called
him *Elvi*. Pawel used the more masculine *E-man*, while Tom Rabbit
called him *The King*. To Kofi, Rainbow's four-year-old son, he was
Elwah. I called him *Bunny*.

Giulia handed me a small flat box wrapped with blue paper.

"Happy early birthday," she said. Inside, a vintage typewriter
key, encased in silver and glass, with the letter *E*.

Some rolled their eyes at my devotion to my dog, but not Giulia.
I clipped the *E* to a blue pendant slung from a leather cord around

my neck. In it, some of Elvis' ashes. I could explain neither the comfort I felt wearing it nor its logic. Along with his fur and bones, which sat next to the bear fetish at home, Elvis' ashes helped me locate myself in the world.

And, I simply wanted him to go everywhere with me. Still.

Giulia and I had rented a house on the mesa outside Taos with a kitchen and a backyard with gas grill and a hot tub. I packed steaks and fat red tomatoes with scallions and anchovies, some cheese and good bread, eggs and tortillas, a couple of bottles of Cava, and some red wine, and planned to warm my skin under the New Mexico sky and perform one last service for my dog: He needed a proper urn—not the overly solemn monoliths made of stone or wood, or the cutesy varieties carved with angels' wings and cherubs that said GOOD BOY, but a container that suited him. Something wild and a little goofy, something surprising, something one of a kind. The edges of Taos were full of pottery outlets stuffed with rows and rooms of ceramics and earthenware advertised with signs proclaiming, 50% SALE *TODAY ONLY!* We would visit them all.

On the first day, we drove to the San Francisco de Assisi Mission, the round adobe church whose transepts look like women's haunches, and whose changing skirts of light were painted by Georgia O'Keeffe. Inside was a chapel for the Virgin de Guadalupe. Giulia lit a candle and said a prayer for motherhood. I've always marveled at how luminous the flames in Catholic churches are: The candles burn with a brightness that goes beyond mere fire.

When I was young, I was convinced the quality of light meant the presence of God.

Outside, I walked over to a shop I knew that sold *retablos* and *milagros,* and found a tiny baby among a dish of icons devoted to common prayers. In it, knees and elbows and hearts, praying figures and homes and livestock. When Giulia joined me, it was clear she had been crying. The adobe ceiling was low, the walls soft and cave-like. Wooden images of saints in all sizes and colors hung floor to ceiling. I pressed the baby into Giulia's palm as she filed through small laminated cards of saints. We decided that St. Gerard Majella—the patron saint of expectant mothers, whose holy handkerchief was said to have helped a woman in a difficult delivery years after his death—was needed. The card with his image came with a prayer to "render me fruitful in offspring."

We stopped at an outlet or two each day—coming back from Abiquiu and Ghost Ranch, or driving out to explore tiny Arroyo Seco—so I could walk the long aisles in search of an urn. I considered brightly colored Talavera and rustic clay pots, black Oaxacan patterns and the ocher-red hues of Mata Ortiz, but nothing fit.

"I was sure it would be here," I said to Giulia over margaritas one night.

On our last full day in Taos, after I'd bought a round pink breast pendant for Giulia on the plaza—"Just in case God is a breast man"—we stopped again at a shop with a handwritten pale blue sign that read JESUS SALE. At first, I'd only wanted a picture, but then I said, "Let's have another look." I must have circled the warehouse twice when I picked up a lime- and pink-colored pot, motioning to Giulia. She turned the round, lidded jar over in her hands and shook her head.

"I'm not sure. Elvis and neon?"

Disappointed, I glanced up over her shoulder, staring at the shapes and colors on the shelves, and glimpsed something hidden behind the rest of the neon pots. In the center of the deep shelving unit stood a tall jug with a banded turquoise top cut with bolt-like squiggles of yellow and pink. Carefully, I fished it out. It was a footed wine jug, with a black gourd-shaped bottom painted with a pink flower, on either side of which were matching doves inscribed in gold. Below the top turquoise portion of the neck was a gold band painted with another flower (white) with pink petals.

I looked around for similar pots.

Nothing.

I opened my mouth to speak, but a wail emerged, a bottomless sound that rose from my gut. The kind shop owner, a round, thick-chested man with a mustache, hurried over.

I shook my head.

"It's for my dog," I said.

He nodded. "I understand."

*   *   *

Back home, the hummingbirds were late. The first females arrived at my feeder the same day word came my mother had suffered a series of small strokes during the procedure Dr. Free had recommended. It was the third week of May. By now I'd been hanging my feeders dutifully for a month. I felt as if I had been holding my breath, waiting to hear them since Elvis died, waiting for the return of joy, the rush of happiness I felt at the first whir on the mountain: the promise of a new season.

As planned, my brother Steve had flown out to be with Mom. I'd spoken to her the night before, but for the first time ever, I wasn't there for the surgery. Steve emailed late in the day to say everything went smoothly, if a bit long. Twelve hours later, there was trouble: Mom was seeing ants on the walls and kittens playing in her food. A whale sailed down the hospital corridor. A CAT scan confirmed strokes, and Mom, on huge doses of prednisone to reduce brain swelling, became so violent, her hands had to be tied to the bed. A neurologist she'd never met prescribed the same medication given to people having a psychotic break.

This would be the beginning of a combative three months. So much had to be done, and every piece of it required a fight—from advocating for my mother in meetings with doctors, caregivers, social workers, and Medicare specialists to trying to figure out what her options were. *Home care or assisted living? Medicare or Medicaid?* As one provider after another contradicted what the previous person had said, we scrambled to formulate a plan and prepare for all eventualities.

For the first time, Dr. Free wasn't optimistic about Mom's recovery. While the new neurologist said Mom "should be just fine," Dr. Free worried about the damage that had been done to her brain over the course of years of repeated coilings. He wasn't sure how much she "would be able to come back from this."

I tried to put a plan in place but ended up charging ahead. I thought I was being efficient; I'd spent so much time taking Mom to doctors, taking notes on her treatments, her medications. I understood best her day-to-day condition. But I ended up ruffling feathers. To my siblings, my efforts read as arrogance and control. I angered far too easily, I was told; I behaved badly if things did not go according to *my plan*. Perhaps it was true. I was operating as an insider treating my siblings as outsiders—they didn't know what I knew and the chip I carried was equal parts experience, exhaustion, and dread about what might come.

In the hospital, Mom was oblivious. Half the time she didn't know her age or the year or where she was. Much worse than her previous stroke. She did, however, remember Barack Obama was president, a historical fact she loved.

"How's Elvis?" she asked me one day as I was visiting.

"Oh, Mom, he died," I said as gently as I could. My mother's face compressed as if she could stop the sudden flush of emotion by cramming her eyes shut and pursing her lips. It was bad enough to hear he was gone, but now the news was compounded by the blank spaces in her memory, the fact that she'd forgotten. I'd seen that look only a couple times over the course of her illness; it was abject fear that she was losing control of her body, her mind. Plus, she'd loved Elvis.

My aunt flew out just as Steve had to return home, and together we worked on plans for all potential futures for Mom. Mary Ann, who was five years younger than my mother, seemed to have grown up in a completely different family; somehow she survived the scorched-earth landscape of her parents' alcoholism with an optimism that I admired. She was the bubbly counterpoint to Mom.

Mary Ann sat with my mother most days and spoke to doctors who showed up whenever it was convenient for them, reporting their comments and Mom's progress in daily emails to the family, while I filled out forms and pressed social workers and the insurance company, and tried to figure out the limits of Medicare coverage. My immediate concern was keeping Mom in a recovery facility long enough for her brain to heal and for her to regain some of her strength and independence. But the insurance company and Medicare could force her out. If they decided to discharge her before she was approved for Medicaid, she'd either have to go into long-term care, for which she did not yet have coverage, or she'd have to live with someone. We held our breath for Medicaid approval so that no matter where Mom landed—home with help or assisted living—there would be a safety net for the services she would require. There was no way to predict what would happen—not the next week, not the next month.

That summer, Mom would retain the threads of herself—unfailing politeness with her caregivers and her taste for potato chips and Diet Pepsi—but the rest would fall away. She had never been much of a fighter, and now, she was clearly beaten. She wanted to, in her words, "be done with it."

In the hospital, Mom's memory was so bad, I had to leave a note taped to her bed tray explaining that she'd had a series of strokes and her memory had been affected. Sometimes she read it and wept. Other times, she pulled at the taped edges and threw it away in the trash, angry, confused.

Over four weeks in June and July, family members rotated in and out after Mom was discharged to home care, but I realized after a few weeks, our plan was not sustainable. It might take six or eight or twelve *months* before my mother could live independently again. Nancy, who had already planned to surprise Mom on her seventieth birthday in July, offered to bring her back to Oregon, where she could live until well enough to return. Relieved, I bought a plane ticket for her to accompany Nancy home. But on the morning of her seventieth birthday, my mother was again rushed to the hospital. Her condition: too tenuous for travel.

My aunt Mary Ann returned, and in a frenzied week of phone calls, meetings, and tours, I gave in to what now, looking back over that long summer, seems like the inevitable: I made arrangements to move my seventy-year-old mother into an assisted living facility.

A week later, as Mom recovered in a care facility for the third time that summer and my aunt took over for me, I drove to the ashram. I was nervous, not knowing what to expect, not interested really in talking to anyone. I wanted to be invisible to the world.

After I checked in and got my key, I asked the slim woman behind the desk, "Who does that dog belong to?" I described the white husky I'd seen disappearing down the path as I walked up the steps—the fluffy coat, the curled tail.

She shook her head. No one at the ashram had a dog like that.

*   *   *

After the first fire ceremony, after yoga and breathing, I met Jimmy, a lanky seventyish Aspenite with a toothy grin. We sat outside at a long picnic table on the deck overlooking a small pond and ate sweet chili tofu with salad in the sun along with the other guests. Jimmy asked about the *Vibhuti* (ash) rubbed into my forehead, a remnant from the *Yajna*.

"They told me it's what's left when everything is burned away," I said, and then described the ceremony.

"Did it work?" he asked.

I shrugged.

We became fast friends, meeting daily for meals and yoga and then a hike. Jimmy was thoughtful and soft-spoken—a dog lover. We shared dog stories and photos: "No wonder you loved him," he said, looking at a picture of Elvis.

I returned to the *Yajna*, compelled. The feeling was like dredging dust long settled into deep grooves. Each morning, I unraveled grief like a cord hooked to my heart and tossed it into the fire. The more *swahas,* the lighter I was.

I'd fought so hard, shoving myself against things, rolling rocks uphill—determination the metal that made me so damn tough. If there was one thing I knew, it was my own strength. But I was beginning to see there was strength in surrender too. Living on Overland Mountain taught me that. The alchemy of wild places is that they work on you the way wind works on rocks, the way twin trickles flowing in opposite directions on Milner Pass high in the Rockies become the Cache la Poudre and the Colorado. The way, a teacher once said, that mantra—*gradually, inevitably*—works on the mind.

Everything else—I let go. *Swaha.*

*   *   *

On our final night at the ashram, I convinced Jimmy to meet me at 2:30 in the morning on the deck of the dining hall to watch the Perseids meteor shower, my favorite August event.

"But the moon is full," he said, smiling.

I waved him off. "It'll be down by then."

When my alarm rang at 2:15, the moon burned with a light equal to day.

Still, Jimmy waited, as promised, on the deck overlooking the lake.

We giggled and giggled. Then I laughed, deep and long.

"They're up there, somewhere," I said, imagining their arrow-like paths and silvery bursts.

"Faith," said Jimmy, nodding.

I told him about the white dog I saw who belonged to no one.

"Do you think it could be Elvis?" I asked.

"I do," he said.

And I believed it. Believing is a choice we make about how we want to see the world. It can be hostile, cold, unkind. Or it can be full of magic. On that day, I believed it was my dog who'd delivered me to this place. That it was his white tail I'd seen disappearing down the trail.

It was time to get on with living.

Chapter 14

A Season of Voluptuousness

Like everyone else on the mountain, I was thinking about the coming fall, larding my calendar with end-of-the-summer chores and observances. August was the month I accepted delivery of four cords of wood and watched the hummingbirds take winter flight. It was also the month when the urgency of the growing season breathed its last, when I cherished each determined bloom in the garden, the stubborn flame of paintbrush in the meadow, the first purple asters—the final flower of the season—poking up between yellowed leaves. My body swung between hurried preparation and manic relaxation: *One more long hike, one more alfresco dinner,* it said, before bad weather and back to school, before the early mornings were perceptibly darker, before the daily lighting of fires commenced.

Into the hourglass of August slipped Greg's unexpected light.

Both shy, reluctant daters, we met online, something I tried on like everyone else, after resisting it for years. My dating history had been a pretty blank sheet marked by a couple of brief affairs and exactly one event that might pass as a "date." Long ago, I'd stopped looking up to catch an interested eye.

I had been half-hopefully, half-distractedly surfing OkCupid for a couple of months—(my justification was a smartly written profile in *The New Yorker* and a burning need to think about anything but Mom)—batting down emails from men who clearly had nothing in common with me, and sending a few tentative hellos, but I hadn't, with one awkward exception, met anyone. The awkward exception turned out to be smart and funny, and worked for the new mayor in Denver. We exchanged a series of witty emails and then one strange and long telephone call. The man peppered me with popcorn-crunching questions about my "remote" conditions only to fall into dumb silence when I described them—bears in the yard, the mouse who just that minute ran down the outside of the stovepipe.

"Wow," he said, "you do live on the edge." After that, his emails abruptly dropped off after he insisted he'd "still like to meet sometime" when he wasn't so busy.

"This," I pronounced as if holding a stinking bag of trash to an ever-encouraging, ever-enthusiastic Giulia, "is a waste of time." Then I got an email addressed to JTG. Jamestown Girl.

In less than a week, ArtDude and I went from short chatty emails to three- and four-hour phone calls. All my life I had been the level-headed one, the go-to girl for friends' relationship woes: "You give such good advice," Giulia said. "You always know what to say."

If I had been me talking to JTG, I would have told her to slow the fuck down.

But JTG did not listen. ArtDude and I fired off a number of emails each day delivering quotidian details: the difference in weather where we were, the peculiarities of our jobs and our schedules paired with an extended discussion of favorite authors and books. Greg was well read, also an artist, a painter of landscapes, a gardener, and a dreamer. He lived in Denver, fifty-five miles away, in a small apartment near Washington Park, and wrote about the way clouds fill the western sky with their own light.

"I have spent a great deal of my life on my back, staring at that sky," he wrote. "I worry I will never be able to capture it. And I worry that I will."

On the sixth morning of wooing, we whipped through nearly two hours of instant messages. As I went off to yoga class, I sent Greg a poem I'd written about a man floating on his back beneath a pier, trying to see the stars in the middle of the day. When I returned, he'd sent a message, confessing in a single line that the poem had made him cry.

"Where did you come from?" he wrote. Then his phone number, in case I "felt like talking."

The voice on the other end was rich and strong. Talking was easy. I felt as if we'd fallen into a slow river. We talked about movies and weather, the American West, westerns, our favorite writers, the view out my window and his. We slipped into conversation easily: There was nothing but recognition and relief.

Almost three hours later, I looked up to realize I had work to do. My classes started the next day. It was as if I'd stepped outside the rushing world.

"I have to go," I said regretfully.

The next day, a Gary Snyder poem showed up in my in-box, part of a daily poetry subscription. It sang of wide-open possibility in the last line: "Everywhere to go." I sent it to Greg.

We spoke every night for the next five, once until well past midnight, when I lay in my bed in the dark, listening to Greg's soothing voice, the phone at my ear, and me whispering, half-awake in the half-light of a waxing moon as coyotes yipped outside. The miller moths were thick that year. Clouds of them greeted me when I returned home in the evening, their gray wings beating against the screen, swarming the deck light. Each night I'd listen to their bodies sizzle and flame in the candles I lit in the bedroom. Like them, I didn't care if I got burned.

All my life I have been skittish about proximity. But I ran toward Greg the way I once ran toward a rim of rock along the Colorado where my rafting group had stopped to cliff-jump. I'd watched from a distance as my best friend sat and hesitated, tiptoed to the edge and tiptoed back. To anyone surveying the scene, I was a bystander. But then I got up—*and ran!*—leaping into the air past the red sandstone edge. I ran that day toward uncertainty, toward something that had equal power to thrill *and* kill me, because I wanted to feel myself a part of air and sky and water, to understand my body as a piece of the natural world and not be afraid.

That same force drew me to Greg. I did not stop to think about shock or temperature, I did not wonder about propriety or safety, I did not dip a tentative toe in or even go gently—instead I plunged.

Greg and I met in Boulder a week and a half after our first email, on a Saturday, driven by burning curiosity and delight, by abject fear mixed with the headiness of all that talking: We'd already confessed too much. Greg had been divorced for ten years and, in his own words, spent the time focused on his son. He was older than me, tall and broad shouldered, with adorable wire-rimmed glasses, black hair combed back from his handsome face. A bit of a cowboy, he wore jeans and lace-up leather boots, a white button-down shirt over a T-shirt even in the eighty-degree heat.

We met at the bus station. He had a leather backpack with his watercolors, a notebook, a copy of Henry Miller's *Black Spring*, a book of Wendell Berry poems, and a clean T-shirt.

"You're not spending the night," I'd warned on the phone the night before in a sudden panic, "let's just see how it goes."

"As you wish," he said.

But it wasn't long before we were plunked down on a blanket in the park along Boulder Creek, and after the fried chicken I'd made and cheese and olives we bought at the farmers' market, after a bit of wine, a bit of chocolate, after some of my poems he'd asked me to bring and read, after kissing there on the grass as kids played in the creek and a tattooed man walked a slack line strung between trees, we fell asleep together, my head on his chest in the warm sun.

Later, Greg would say he had the feeling of being located at the center of a map beneath a fat arrow that said YOU ARE HERE pointing to our bodies on the grass.

"The rest of the world," he said, "the cyclists and skaters, the people sitting on the grass, swirled all around. Only we were still."

We lay there until the shadows spread out over the park, then drove up the winding apron of Left Hand to James Canyon and beyond to Overland. Amazingly, Greg had spent some time at Balarat, a camp halfway between the cabin and Jamestown, when he was in high school. As we drove, he talked about throwing his sleeping bag down in a meadow for the night and waking to deer grazing all around.

"I'll never forget that feeling," he said. "I just lay still and watched for the longest time."

Greg sat out on the deck watching the birds at the feeder as I stretched pizza dough and sprinkled arugula with lemon and truffle oil for a salad. He rose from his seat when I brought out flutes of Cava laced with Chambord. There was a bit of old world about him: He opened doors and called strangers sir and ma'am; he carried a cloth handkerchief in his back pocket, which he offered when I sneezed. He was a true gentleman; his kindness and manners were tied to a moral compass, a way of perceiving and acting in the world, absolutely without guile or agenda. I thought he was the nicest man I'd ever met.

I put the doughs on the grill and we ate a bubbled and crusty pizza Margherita and another with sliced Honeycrisp apples dotted with Gorgonzola cheese. The salad held bits of shaved Parmesan and crushed hazelnuts.

"Wow," said Greg, who later confessed he thought my food was a bit "fancy."

Afterward, I put my feet up in his lap, in a gesture that felt as comfortable in its implied intimacy as it was surprising. As we watched the sun sink behind the Indian Peaks, Greg took each foot and rubbed it. His hands were strong, his touch solid, not tentative.

He left two days later.

The storyteller Clarissa Pinkola Estés tells the tale of Skeleton Woman, a woman who has been cast by her father into the ocean until one day she is caught by a fisherman, who, terrified at her wild hair and bony appearance, paddles furiously away and then runs home, all the while thinking he is being chased by the apparition whose rib is snared by his hook. Misunderstanding the nature of her "pursuit," he runs and runs, carrying his rod with him, chased by the terrifying woman until both collapse inside his igloo. After a while, he takes pity on her convoluted form, and singing to her, he gently unwinds the tangles of line and bone and wraps her in fur and then falls asleep. In the night, the man dreams and a tear draws down his face and Skeleton Woman puts her bony lips to it and drinks, quenching what was said to be a long, long thirst. Then she reaches inside his chest and takes out his heart, chanting "Flesh! Flesh! Flesh!" as her bones grow muscle and her muscle grows flesh, until she is a woman again with breasts and hands and skin. Then she lies beside the man and sleeps, and in the morning, they wake, entangled, as if it had always been that way.

Greg and I shared that familiarity, a sense that even though we'd just met, we'd known each other for a long, long time. I suppose this is the feeling that makes lovers. Suddenly the story you are living is bigger than you.

When I returned home on Monday night, after dropping Greg at the bus station that morning, after teaching and yoga, I found an ink drawing tucked next to my pillow. On it, a man and a woman holding hands on top of a mountain, looking up at the stars.

In this way, we plunged into the fall, to me the most voluptuous season, for its urgent last-ditch displays of color and chilly, smoke-scented evenings. I've always thought that life was the richest not in the first messy blush of spring but there, on the edge of decay. There's a profound and undeniable sensuality in death just as there is in birth: The body labors to leave this life just as a body labors to give it. I have seen it myself. In my own life, Greg would provide the counterpoint to my mother's tortuously slow decline. Our relationship was the answer to her waning light.

Earlier, I'd begun the heartbreaking process of paring down my mother's life, reducing her possessions to what could fit in an eight-by-eleven room. Together, Greg and I moved a handful of Mom's things into the Mary Sandoe House at the foot of the Boulder Flatirons, a facility with modern and cozy living spaces and single rooms. It was an oasis in an otherwise putrid field of choices for people on Medicaid—decrepit facilities decorated predominantly in laminate and taupe, and smelling too often of urine.

Although I would continue to hope for the best through fall and winter, by spring it would be clear my mother was diminished. She complained she was too weak to go on outings to the grocery store or library. And although I'd asked her doctor to order more physical therapy and encouraged Mom to walk and participate in activities—a gentle exercise class, bingo, watercolor painting—even then, her mind was made up. She'd begun to slowly fade from the world, receding into the silence of her room, watching television all day long.

I didn't see it then. I was still too busy trying to hold her up. We spoke every day on the phone, and often, I delivered what I called the Monday Night special—dinner from KFC or Good Times, which my mother loved. But by the Fourth of July, ten months after she'd moved into assisted living, she would be noticeably weaker, slower to dress. It would take Greg and me ten full minutes to get her from her room to the picnic area outside where residents had gathered for a barbecue. Once there, Mom was delighted to eat things not on the healthy menu at the house: burgers and hot dogs and potato salad, cupcakes and pie—the happiest I'd seen her in a while.

As Greg helped serve plates of dessert to residents, Mom tugged on my shirt.

"He's a good man," she said.

My favorite picture of my mother was taken on that day. In it, she is wearing my weathered white cowboy hat. Her mouth is open, her face tilted up as she laughs at one of Greg's jokes.

I look at that picture often, remembering her happy—before more ER visits, before more aching and drawn-out decline, before the day six months later when she would be admitted to the hospital with pneumonia and then diagnosed with respiratory failure. After weeks in the ICU, after her doctor suggested still more tests to see why she was not recovering, after her diagnosis—"failure to thrive"—I would hear my mother pronounce a firm, unequivocal *No,* for the first time in her life.

"I'm done," she said.

And although she would be released to hospice, she would languish for another two full years in a nursing home, never to leave her bed again.

I would visit the foul-smelling facility delivering Mom's weekly cupcakes because by now my mother refused dietary restrictions in addition to all medications. I was told it wasn't uncommon for people who went on hospice to rally, as my mother did the morning after I'd said my final goodbye, when I'd walked into her room to see her sitting upright eating potato chips. Mom would live the rest of her days blissfully unaware of where she was. For the first time, there was no struggle.

"You're my angel," she'd say to me. "I don't know what I would do without you."

"I love you, sweetie," she would say. Every single time.

A final gift. My mistake had been in stubbornly trying to get her to love me on my terms, not hers. There was nothing more I could do for her. Mom's life had been hard, but now everything had been pared away.

"Thanks, Mom," I said. "I love you too."

She told me, "I wish I could go back to when you were a child and raise you differently. You deserved better."

She died a few months later, after I fed her her last meal: three sips of Pepsi.

But all of this was in a future I could not yet see, in a story that would unfold itself, at times achingly, as my mother reveled in being cared for, as together we waited for death.

*   *   *

By the time the first snow fell on the mountain, Greg and I had long since professed our love, reserving most Friday to Sundays for the pleasure of each other's embrace. We read poetry to each other, picnicked in front of the woodstove, and had lazy Sundays in bed with coffee and *The New York Times*. Between visits, we talked on the phone every single night, sending smoke signals to each other across the distance. I wrote poems and morning emails, Greg sent texts when I was in town. We exchanged letters. In between, I continued to look after Mom: My pendulum swung between empty and full.

Still, I carried the weight of new love clumsily at times, unused to considering another's point of view. In October, I thought it would be lovely and romantic to camp in the desert with Greg, but he had a million reasons not to go: *It was too soon for a trip together, he wasn't ready, Moab was the place he went with his ex-wife*. So I went alone. Chalk it up to an old sense of indignation and my penchant for displays of independence. I was still me.

At night I dreamed of bears, menacing, trying to get inside a glass house. I dreamed of Elvis, old or living with people who did not take care of him. I dreamed of myself as a shambling creature who, even though I spoke, could not be understood. In the dream,

I lost words, the ability to communicate, and was treated savagely. Misunderstood, I could only threaten with my physical presence. This new world felt strange. I did not know its language.

I missed my dog, I missed Greg. Then, unexpectedly, I got a call from him on my cell while I was strolling the streets of Moab my last night.

"I know I'm not supposed to call," he said, "but I miss you."

"Me too," I said, amazed at how happy I was to hear his voice.

As winter settled on the mountain, the quiet without Greg had texture and presence. I missed him. Our weekends together had become a haven from the weight of the season, from the two-hour round-trip to deliver food to Mom, from a four-day, five-class teaching load that took me in opposite directions along the Front Range. To my surprise, I slept better when Greg was with me, his body the anchor I needed. When he wasn't there, I sometimes phoned after a bad early-morning dream, and he would stop painting and crawl back into his own bed, gently talking me back to sleep.

Even the snow felt like drudgery, but Greg made the work of winter lighter. He shoveled and split wood. He stocked the wood box for me and put seed out for the birds. We spent a few snow days almost entirely in bed, the fire fueled by the results of Greg's labor. Once, he drove up to stock my wood box because I'd hurt my back.

In February, we celebrated a T. S. Eliot dedicated to "Incendiary Things."

Greg spent the day oiling the wood coffee table and later filled the cabin with tea lights that flickered on every surface. Outside, he lined the walkway with the same radiant flames embedded in snow. Mountain luminarias.

I kissed him. "Beautiful."

"No, incendiary," he said.

My friends arrived, with the noticeable absence of Judith, who had moved to Boulder and out of the house she'd shared for twenty-five years with David.

"I can't believe something that seemed so good could go so wrong," I said to Greg.

He shrugged. "Being in a relationship is like being naked, on a handcart in a tunnel in a mine, racing into the dark." He was okay with the uncertainty, I was not. That night, my friends were at their naughtiest—Jac supplied the limericks, and Giulia, dressed in a flowing red skirt and black boa, led us in a rousing game of Bullshit. Greg supplied the music—Shakira, Patti Smith, The Replacements. When it was time for dessert, I asked everyone to blow out the candles as I lit a pool of cognac at the top of the volcano-shaped Baked Alaska I'd made. Delicate flames traced lavalike paths down the sides, making a beautiful light in the cabin.

*   *   *

Spring arrived trumpeting a kind of urgency down in Boulder. Daffodils and crocus exploded, while on the mountain, the lilacs bloomed full and rich. At night, I listened to a mouse, though it sounded like something far bigger, flipping papers in the crawl space above my bed. Nesting? One morning, I woke to saltine crackers hidden inside my Uggs, on another, I noticed the peach-colored feather boa Judith had given me for my birthday a few years back was chewed to a rat's tail at one end.

"How big *are* you?" I said out loud. Out came the traps.

The bears returned, walking the edges of my property in a way they hadn't in years, perhaps sensing the dog was now gone. One chilly, rain-filled night, I was awakened by a bruin politely unscrewing the hummingbird feeder bottom from its glass top. I'd lazily left it out after a day full of rain. *No bears tonight,* I'd thought, but I'd reckoned wrongly.

"Hey!" I yelled out the window, getting up and going into the mushy yard to shoo the bear away and unhook the feeders.

I'll confess I'd started to count the months with Greg, ticking them off like signposts on the road to a certain destination. *How long could we last?* Every spat, every misunderstanding became an occasion to evaluate the long-term possibility of our relationship. I didn't trust happiness. Compromise came hard. I filed each quarrel under *something to worry about* or *reasons we will not work out.*

Nevertheless, summer arrived. Greg planted a shade-tolerant rosebush in the spot where I'd tried to get lavender and coreopsis to grow and helped me dig aspen roots to make room for Colorado natives like penstemon and blanketflower. We shared happy hours with my new seasonal Nebraska neighbors, Sandi and Randy, on the deck of their house overlooking the High Lake and went to the Merc for brunch.

Rainbow, who'd bought the Merc when Joey retired the year before, had infused it with her own creative and funky sensibility by pulling the bar back and getting rid of the pie case that had stopped working decades ago and redoing the rotting kitchen floor. She put fruit trees in the windows and changed the menu to include avocados and big salads and instructed the cooks to hand-cut fries. Now there were three kinds of Benedicts on the Sunday menu and real sirloin burgers. In July, she asked me to participate in *2 Dollar Radio*, an "old-time radio show" to be recorded at and produced by the Merc. Hosted by a former Jamestown musician, the show was part *eTown*, part *Prairie Home Companion*.

It was a chilly, drizzly summer Sunday and the Merc was lined with rows of chairs facing the front, toward the window, which was fogged over, glowing with the twinkling white lights added to Joey's colored Christmas string. Greg sat next to me wearing a pearl-buttoned western shirt and cowboy hat. We laughed along with everyone else as Snake delivered the "Jamestown News" in a rambling, off-the-cuff monologue that announced among other things that "a millionaire bought a mountain and is going to make us all rich," referring to the purchase of the Burlington Mine on the edge of town for gold exploration. Kristen, a petite dark-haired beauty, read the weather: "Summer will arrive on July first and depart on July twenty-fifth." Joey hammed it up on the microphone, playing "When I'm Sixty-Four" on his kazoo. Rainbow read a couple of favorite poems, and I introduced the Bachelor of the Month, *2 Dollar Radio*'s attempt "to curb the rampant problem of mountain bachelors." Last, the Tiny Penny Award, meant to "recognize an act of tiny acclaim," was given out by Sarah, who announced in her itty-bitty voice that Adam the Lifeguard had run to his house for a tool needed at the Merc, "a small deed that otherwise might have gone unnoticed."

The town had gathered to celebrate its quirkiness and to poke fun at itself, but unlike the plays or musical events or even the three-ring circus of the Fourth of July, which tended toward excess in every possible way, there was a sweetness to this afternoon. Everyone genuinely enjoyed each other. Afterward, as Greg and I stood talking to other audience members, gushing about what we were certain was the best thing we'd ever seen in Jamestown, I remembered the arrow Greg had described, locating us on the map: *You are here.*

Yes, I thought.

* * *

In August, we lay on top of my open sleeping bag in the middle of the road behind my cabin in the only patch of open ground watching the Perseids. Greg was nervous about a car surprising us even though I assured him that was unlikely—especially at 2:00 A.M.

"Only locals drive here."

The ground was still warm from the day and two great horned owls called back and forth across the meadow. I was sleepy and after a while, curled toward Greg's chest, pulling the edges of the bag around me. He would return to Denver in the morning. For now, we seemed content to go back and forth. Missing each other was part of our call and response.

The smell of dirt was all around. I could reach out and rub my fingers in it. I was sinking into a new life, one still rich with uncertainty. We shared place the same way we shared kisses—the mountain, the seasons, the stars were ours. Greg was not the piece that made me whole, or my reward for all the years I spent alone. But here at last I could see the love story—how I'd learned what it meant to be in relationship: with place, with people, with myself. I no longer needed to walk away. Instead, I would walk to. I loved the mountain and I loved him: We were meant to love each other for as long and as hard as we could.

The Fox Who Came to Dinner

G reg and I celebrated the anniversary of our meeting on the night a fox I'd seen in the spring tentatively nosed her way onto the deck, toward the smell of grilled lamb. We toasted each other and watched the stars appear one by one as we tossed the meaty bones out into the yard for our visitor.

She'd first shown up on another anniversary—Elvis' death— when I put out a bit of chicken in memory of my dog. Since then, I'd spied fox scat on the rocks near the steps, a calling card.

Through the fall, perhaps persuaded by the leftovers I scattered whenever I saw her, Little Girl, as I now called her, became a reg- ular guest. A few evenings a week, she showed up, setting off the motion-sensor light on the deck outside, and out I'd come, with whatever leftovers I had in hand. From the yard, she looked at me with the big unblinking eyes of a Victorian beggar.

There were a million reasons not to feed the fox, the least of which were the bigger predators she might attract. But it was too late. She'd developed a habit of sitting on the deck at the top of the steps, just as Elvis had, watching the yard from her perch. I looked forward to her visits and, ridiculously, worried she didn't have enough food.

Then one day in the frozen cold of January, Little Girl limped into the yard with a lame back foot.

"She'll probably be okay," said the youngish-sounding volunteer at the wildlife rehabilitation center, before adding nonchalantly, "she'll survive or she won't." They would trap her only if she became immobile.

That's when I started feeding the fox in earnest.

Little Girl loved raw eggs and raw chicken, turning her nose up at filler foods like rice and potatoes. The nights were so cold that food left out froze instantly. So each evening, I waited devotedly for the porch light to come on and out I'd go with a plate of her favorites, which I laid gently on the steps as she waited just beyond my reach.

By the time she recovered, I was buying two dozen eggs a week and stocking my freezer with family packs of chicken legs. On a couple of nights when she didn't show up, I went barefoot into the snow to call her name.

It was another desperate and cold winter. When I'd moved to Overland Mountain with my dog, nearly a decade before, I had gone days without speaking to another person. That had changed with Greg. And even though we talked each night on the phone, the distance had begun to make him feel like a part-time lover. I missed him achingly when he wasn't around. The fox eased the lonesomeness, along with the sharper edge of the season.

As winter finally thawed into spring, Little Girl started losing her coat in unruly, irregular clumps. By now she'd made a regular day bed on the rock outcropping outside and I could see her itching furiously and biting at her ratlike tail.

She had mange.

Again, the wildlife rehabilitation people were unsympathetic. "It's common," they said, and they rarely treated it.

This would never do: I ordered a homeopathic remedy from a fox rescue organization in England and, as instructed, dutifully sprinkled it on peanut butter and honey sandwiches. I dosed the fox for the full four weeks, even arranging to have Rainbow feed her when I had to go out of town.

Pasque flowers gave way to Indian paintbrush on the mountain, and Little Girl stopped itching, shedding her winter coat to reveal silky red summer fur. Her tail grew back, bushy and full. It was then in the dusk of a summer evening, as Little Girl stepped tentatively onto the deck, that I noticed "she" was a "he."

"I guess it's Little One now," said Greg on the phone.

Still, the fox showed up each night—now later with the setting sun—to eat his plate of food: first the eggs, carrying one off into the woods before returning for the other. I'd see him burying them at the foot of a tree, sometimes in my own yard. Then he'd return for the chicken leg, eating it at the foot of the steps. Once or twice he stuck his nose inside the open screen door of my cabin and I had to shoo him away.

He had become part of my landscape.

In July, Giulia announced that she was pregnant at long last, and in August, Greg and I camped together for the first time, exploring a couple of ghost towns in the Collegiate Peaks and reading each other poetry with coffee and a campfire in the mornings. When we celebrated another anniversary at the hot springs in Buena Vista, I was sure it was time to take a step closer. But we squabbled about location and logistics, in love with our respective places. I refused to leave the mountain, he the city.

And then, as it had so many times, the landscape shifted.

Not three weeks later, a week of persistent and heavy September rains dropped twenty inches of water on the mountain and forced Jim Creek to swell well past spring runoff heights. At night, the disconcerting sound of boulders booming as they collided in the creek could be heard in Jamestown, and the Little Jim, the seasonal trickle that ran by the road up to Overland, filled to five times its size and speed, significantly widening its banks. The world was soggy. Water gushed down the sides of the canyon and ran along the road. Instinctively, on the fifth day of nonstop rain, I returned home early after a university meeting instead of running errands in town.

Not ten hours later, Jamestown became the confluence of three twenty-foot-deep rivers: Jim Creek, the Little Jim to the west, and the drainage off Gillespie Spur on the southern edge of town. Just before midnight, a mudslide loosed itself from the top of Porphyry Mountain above Jamestown and slammed with the force of a semi barreling down the highway at eighty miles an hour into Joey's house on Main Street, shoving the house off its foundation and killing Joey instantly. His housemate, Miles, survived and scrambled across the street to Nancy Farmer's, pounding on the door for her to wake up—probably saving lives. Until his 911 call, no one understood the gravity of the situation. The road below Joey's was blocked by the turbulent and deadly waters of the mudslide. Someone's car floated, along with whole trees and propane tanks, on the swollen belly of James Creek.

My phone rang at 1:30 A.M. It was Karen Z, reporting that half her yard was gone and the creek raged just a foot below her bridge-driveway.

"Get in your truck now and get up here," I said, then posted on the town message board that my house was open for anyone who could get to higher ground. I didn't know then that the road leading up Overland had been cut off by another massive slide on the western side. Escape from Jamestown was blocked on both ends. And the town was divided down the middle, into north and south halves, by the flood that rushed over Main Street and carved out vast chunks of blacktop. Before rescue helicopters would land two days later, a third of the homes in town, including Karen Z's and Nancy Farmer's, which crumpled accordion-like into the creek, were washed away. The little park across from the Merc where the horseshoers gathered on warm days and where Jamestown hosted its Fourth of July pancake breakfast vanished, replaced by a rubble field of downed pines and boulders, and Ward Street, where I'd first lived in Jamestown when Elvis was just three, was scraped to bedrock—the road base now six feet *below* the driveways of the homes there. Houses on Main Street and Lower Main were gutted with six feet of sand, and the town, without water, without electricity, without access, was all but uninhabitable. And would be for months.

Up on Overland, at the highest point on the mountain, I still had four inches of standing water on the ground and was stranded without power or a way off the mountain for five days. Our communication cut off, Greg was frantic. I walked down Overland along the thirty-foot-wide chasm carved by the Little Jim to the western edge of Jamestown to survey the damage but was stopped by twenty feet of roiling creek instead of road. A man called from the other side of the gorge, saying final evacuations were beginning. My friends—Rainbow, Adam, and their kids; and Judith, who'd recently moved into a basement apartment just down-canyon, along with nearly two hundred other Jamestown residents—had already been flown out as part of what was to be the largest airlift rescue since Hurricane Katrina. A handful of Jimtowners, including Kathleen and her husband, Vic, who lived high on the hill on the northern ridge of town, and Karen Z, who volunteered to take care of pets left behind, stubbornly remained, unwilling to abandon the town. They would ration their food for weeks until the slides were cleared and the road leading up Overland was repaired.

I spent one fall weekend with Sandi and Randy, diving into the carcass of Karen Z's house, the bulk of which dangled and spilled in Jim Creek like a cast-off sack of trash, searching for a few precious things, including an antique diamond ring that had belonged to Karen's mother. Later, along with other volunteers, I salvaged what I could from her still-standing kitchen and carted it to her shed. Eventually she would have to let the bank foreclose on the remaining three walls of her kitchen, and start over in another house built by the Mennonite relief services near the lower park. It would be three years before she had a home of her own again.

For the next six weeks, I would drive a circuitous hour-and-a-half-long route across the Peak to Peak Highway to twenty miles of rutted dirt road through Gold Hill before a less onerous, but still long, alternative route opened through Nederland, down to Boulder and beyond. It would be nine months until a temporary and primitive "locals only" road would open in James Canyon, and I hazarded being stopped by the sheriff because I lived in the wrong zip code. But I *was* a local. It's true the route saved time, but truer was that it was strange not to pass through Jamestown on my way up or down the canyon, even stranger not to see so many familiar faces as I did.

That winter the fox's coat bloomed full and glorious. Greg painted a watercolor of him sitting on the tall rocks just outside my kitchen window and gave it to me for Christmas. Some mornings I woke up to the fox's tracks in the snow as I was filling the feeders and he'd come bounding up, dropping down from a place where he'd bedded nearby.

In the spring, Giulia gave birth to a round and beautiful baby girl who had a magnificent shock of black hair. At the same time, my sister announced she was returning home to Colorado. The fox's appearances grew scarce. *He has a family now,* I thought, figuring he had to be about three years old and should have mated long ago. In April, I didn't see even his tracks in the yard, and by the time I'd come home from an extended trip in May, my life had been foxless for a full six weeks. I spied a fox farther down-canyon, about a mile from my house, but I couldn't be sure it was him.

Along with the birds, more and more Jamestown residents migrated back with spring thaw. Cisterns popped up in yards while residents waited out construction of a new town water system. That year the Fourth of July was marked by a small party in the big park featuring a kazoo band in honor of Joey. Some say the best one ever. I made fried chicken with the chicken legs stored for the fox in the freezer and invited Nancy, her husband, and my niece to celebrate the rainy day with Greg and me on the deck of my cabin. Still, I missed the fox and tried not to think that they live an average of four years in the wild.

Yet the world fills in the gaps it makes. Four months after Elvis died, I met Greg, and four months after I last saw the fox, Greg and I made hopeful plans for a home together.

For almost two months we scoured the mountain and watched one by one as our prospects failed. I expanded our search to the flatlands. Although what happened was not directly precipitated by the flood, the event engineered an outcome nonetheless. Because a "hundred-year event" had scrubbed the canyons up and down the Front Range, mountain homes were scarce.

I cried the day we signed our lease for a house on the edge of a sprawling prairie town and every day thereafter as I packed my things. But I knew in my heart it was the thing to do. I'd have to let go of one landscape to enter another. The faith that told me the fox found a vixen and they moved to better territory for them and their family was the same faith that said the new territory I was entering with Greg, unfamiliar in so many ways, was a better place for us, together.

The first snow arrived on the mountain the day in late September that Greg and I loaded the moving truck. Wet aspen leaves littered the walk and the monkshood, which had bloomed at last, slumped to the ground. Overnight, the season had changed.

While Greg waited in the drive, I stood on the deck one last time, my view of Indian Peaks obscured, and then walked down the steps to stand in the garden.

The geode I'd salvaged from the fire still sat on the twisted, heart-shaped stump, as it had every day since I'd moved in. For forty seasons, the flat-faced stone had been my talisman: *The rock had survived and so would I*. At first, I thought to keep it as a reminder of my resilience—but real strength, I'd come to realize, lies not in resistance but in softness, the willingness to go unguarded into a new day. Looking at the cloudy face, I remembered the words of Gretel Ehrlich: "To know something, then, we must be scrubbed raw, the fasting heart exposed." I had wanted all along to know my place. Now I knew the contours of my own heart.

As chickadees twittered in the trees, I breathed the cool mountain air. The next day Nancy Farmer, who'd been living in an apartment outside Boulder since the flood, would move into the cabin, returning after more than a year off the mountain.

I left the inscrutable rock face up on the stump. My story was part of the Overland Mountain now: *I know what the world is made of, and I still love all of it.*

Finally, it was time to go.

Acknowledgments

First thanks goes to Peter Catapano of *The New York Times,* who plucked me from decades of writing obscurity when he published my fox story in "Menagerie" and opened the door for all manner of good things.

Gratitude isn't a big enough word for the miracle of Bonnie Solow, my agent, who appeared out of the blue and is, first and foremost, a kindred spirit. Her instinct, passion, and particular brand of gusto are manna from heaven. Thank you for your wise counsel and for loving the fox and Elvis and me.

At Scribner, Shannon Welch's keen eye shaped the story and helped make a memoir from a collection of essays. Kathy Belden offered gentle prodding on critical passages. Nan Graham provided the light and the last word. Thank you all. And to the rest of my Scribner team, including the fabulous Sally Howe and my publicist Kate Lloyd, along with every single person working diligently to make this book—so much gratitude and many coupes de champagne.

So many people helped, supported, and cheered my writing on over the years that I must mention a few of them who have kept my feet stubbornly on the road. Among them, at the University of Colorado, Peter Michelson, the best guest at any dinner party and a great man who never once pulled a punch with me. He, along with the poet Lorna Dee Cervantes, first believed. To Reg Saner, who planted the seed of nonfiction, and Lucia Berlin, who in her own circuitous way taught me to believe in myself. To Michael Wilson at the University of Wisconsin–Milwaukee, who saw me as both writer and colleague. Fellow writers David Gessner, Nina De Gramont, Burns "Sweetie" Ellison, and Big Jim Campbell formed my first writing community, and their friendship and support have sustained me over the years. Final inspiration comes from the women in my summer workshops on Overland Mountain, whose willingness so often kept the fires of my work burning—especially Laura Marshall, Jan Reed, Nancy Farmer, and JoAnna Rotkin. Thank you, Oak, Nancy E, Jeannie, Kelly, Helen, Giulia, and all of the writers who came to practice and play. To Jacqueline Herlihy, who has been with me from the start and is the best copy editor I know.

Two friendships have sustained me and made me a better writer and a happier human being. Both have provided not only kinship and poetry but a bit of necessary bawdiness, a deep love of the sensual, and an abiding and enthusiastic keenness for words. To resident rock star and partner in crime Oody Petty, my hero, and to Helen Turner, a wild soul who will always and forever dance to her own bighearted tune, I love you both.

I am indebted to those who took time to read and comment on

this manuscript as I wrote and rewrote: first Helen and Oody, then my aunt Mary Ann Auvinen McGaughey and my sister, Nancy: huge thanks. The book in your hands would not be possible without the immense generosity and superhuman diligence of Elizabeth Geoghegan, who read and commented on every chapter from her remove in Rome while teaching half a dozen classes, and urged me—always—to keep going. An ocean of gratitude, my colleague, my friend.

Thank you also to the places that supported me while I wrote: the Jentel Foundation in beautiful wide-open Wyoming for Marilyn the cat and the lovely firelit studio, and to the artist Pilar Hanson for the long walks toward the horizon while we figured it all out. Thank you to the Marquez family for the cabin that provided long hours of concentration as I edited and to the Java Moose in Fairplay, Colorado, for a good lunch, a bit of electricity, and Wi-Fi when I came up for air. Thank you to Sandi and Randy for their lovely High Lake home and Jean and Helen for retreats along the way.

To the people of Jamestown who came to the rescue when I lost everything, especially Kara and Waldy Baumgart, my generous friend and trail buddy Karen Z, Bonnie Maddalone, Nancy Edelstein, Jean Hofve, Holly Smith-Mann, the late Joey Howlett, and all the Jamestown Mercantile regulars. For giving me a home in Jamestown: Helen and Allan. For love and support when I needed it the most: Rainbow and Adam. For a lifetime of friendship and ritual: Jolene

Kindig. Thank you to my High Lake neighbors who first showed me that no one does it alone: Joe and Kathy, and Paul and Teresa.

And finally, so much heart for Greg Marquez, who generously painted the interior watercolors for the book, read every draft, and abided so many "quiet mornings" as I wrote. Your love has been a ladder to the stars. I know your aim is true.

Author's Note

I have tried here to tell the story that I know about my life and my childhood. My family, who did not ask to be written about, have their own tales to tell. To them, I offer love and understanding that we each have a story and a part to play.

Last, what I know to be true about mountain towns is this: People not described in these pages will see themselves, and to them, I apologize. For the rest who are, I have exchanged names and faces and obfuscated out of respect for the urge for anonymity that pushes people to the hills.